Ghoncheh Tazmini is an Iranian-born independent political analyst who has worked with research institutes in Europe and Iran. Educated at the University of British Columbia and the London School of Economics, she holds a PhD in International Relations from the University of Kent at Canterbury. She is Research Director at the Ravand Institute for Economic and International Studies.

International Library of Iranian Studies

See www.ibtauris.com/ILIS for a full list of titles

1. *Converting Persia: Religion and Power in the Safavid Empire*
Rula Abisaab
978 1 86064 970 7

2. *Iran and the World in the Safavid Age*
Willem Floor and Edmund Herzig (eds)
978 1 85043 930 1

3. *Religion and Politics in Modern Iran: A Reader*
Lloyd Ridgeon
978 1 84511 073 4

4. *The Qajar Pact: Bargaining, Protest and the State in Nineteenth-Century Persia*
Vanessa Martin
978 1 85043 763 5

5. *The Fire, the Star and the Cross: Minority Religions in Medieval and Early Modern Iran*
Aptin Khanbaghi
978 1 84511 056 7

6. *Allopathy Goes Native: Traditional Versus Modern Medicine in Iran*
Agnes Loeffler
978 1 85043 942 4

7. *Iranian Cinema: A Political History*
Hamid Reza Sadr
978 1 84511 146 5

8. *Sasanian Persia: The Rise and Fall of an Empire*
Touraj Daryaee
978 1 85043 898 4

9. *In the Shadow of the King: Zill al-Sultan and Isfahan under the Qajars*
Heidi A. Walcher
978 1 85043 434 4

10. *Decline and Fall of the Sasanian Empire: The Sasanian-Parthian Confederacy and the Arab Conquest of Iran*
Parvaneh Pourshariati
978 1 84511 645 3

11. *The Forgotten Schools: The Baha'is and Modern Education in Iran, 1899–1934*
Soli Shahvar
978 1 84511 683 5

12. *Khatami's Iran: The Islamic Republic and the Turbulent Path to Reform*
Ghoncheh Tazmini
978 1 84511 594 4

13. *Revolutionary Ideology and Islamic Militancy: The Iranian Revolution and Interpretations of the Quran*
Najibullah Lafraie
978 1 84511 063 5

14. *Becoming Visible in Iran: Women in Contemporary Iranian Society*
Mehri Honarbin-Holliday
978 1 84511 878 5

15. *Tribeswomen of Iran: Weaving Memories among Qashqa'i Nomads*
Julia Huang
978 1 84511 832 7

16. *Islam and Dissent in Post-revolutionary Iran: Abdolkarim Soroush, Religious Politics and Democratic Reform*
Behrooz Ghamari-Tabrizi
978 1 84511 879 2

17. *Persia in Crisis: Safavid Decline and the Fall of Isfahan*
Rudi Matthee
978 1 84511 745 0

18. *Blogistan: The Internet and Politics in Iran*
A. Srebeny and G. Khiabany
978 1 84511 606 4

19. *Christian Encounters with Iran: Engaging Muslim Thinkers after the Revolution*
Sasan Tavassoli
978 1 84511 761 0

KHATAMI'S IRAN

The Islamic Republic and the Turbulent Path to Reform

GHONCHEH TAZMINI

TAURIS ACADEMIC STUDIES
an imprint of

I.B.Tauris Publishers
LONDON • NEW YORK

Published in 2009 by Tauris Academic Studies
An imprint of I.B.Tauris & Co Ltd
6 Salem Road, London W2 4BU
175 Fifth Avenue, New York NY10010
www.ibtauris.com

Distributed in the United States and Canada
Exclusively by Palgrave Macmillan
175 Fifth Avenue, New York NY 10010

International Library of Iranian Studies 12

ISBN 978 1 84511 594 4

A full CIP record for this book is available from the British Library
A full CIP record for this book is available from the Library of Congress

Library of Congress catalog card: available

Printed and bound in India by Thomson Press (India)
Camera-ready copy edited and supplied by the author

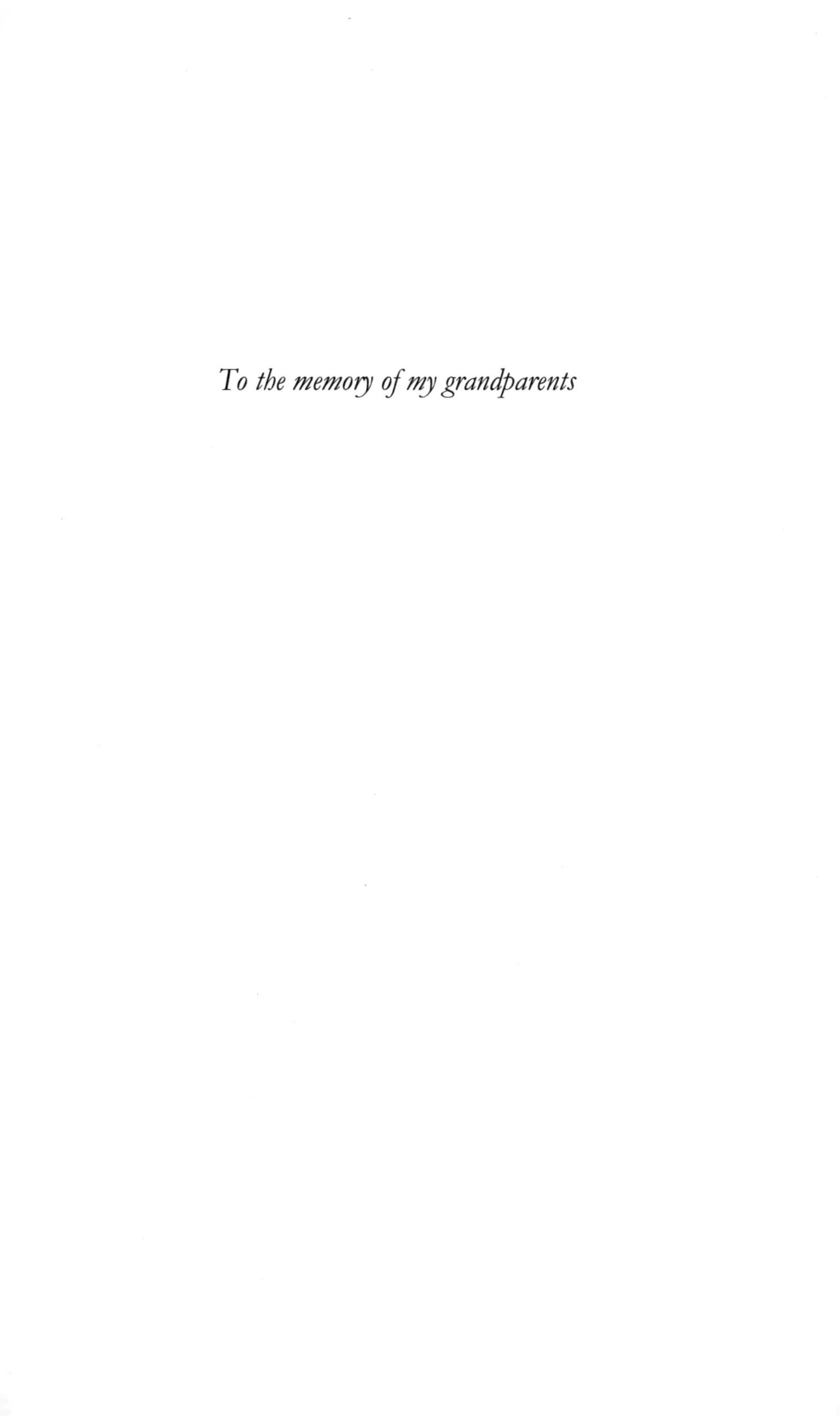

To the memory of my grandparents

CONTENTS

ACKNOWLEDGEMENTS

This book is the product of a collective effort. The complexity of the subject matter, and my determination to weave it into an analytic, yet accessible narrative proved to be a challenging and at times daunting task. I certainly could not have completed it without the support of colleagues, family and friends. The debts incurred in producing this book are numerous. First, I would like to thank Seyyed Mohammad Khatami for his time and valuable thoughts. On the various occasions that I had the pleasure of speaking with him, I found him to be an intelligent man with an engaging personality. While I would have liked to have discussed this work with him more extensively, I had to wrestle to maintain arm's length distance in order to maintain an academic balance to my work. I would like to thank his associates, particularly Mr. Sadegh Kharazi. The project benefited greatly from the guidance and moral support of Mr. Mohammad Taheri, and the scholarly expertise of Dr. Mohammad Javad Faridzadeh. I owe a great deal to the reflections of Mr. Parviz Mansouri, for without them the original idea of this book would never have been conceived.

The subtle comments and criticisms of many experts who read my work proved invaluable. Among them were Dr. Richard Sakwa, Dr. Mohsen Milani, Dr. Mohiaddin Mesbahi and Dr. Hossein Adeli. Dr. Reza Davari-Ardakani's insights immensely benefited my work. I would like to thank Dr. Ali Reza Sheikholislami for his helpful advice in the preparation of this book. I always received valuable research assistance from the wonderful staff of the Library of the Institute for Political and International Studies of the Iranian Ministry of Foreign Affairs. I am also grateful to Iradj Bagherzade,

Joanna Godfrey, Elizabeth Munns, Rasna Dhillon, Arnold Ross, Clare Thomlinson, Susan Forsyth and the anonymous readers for their efforts in helping me sharpen my final draft and in getting my manuscript into print.

My greatest indebtedness is to my parents, Mohammad Ali and Sousan, and my sister, Ghazaleh. I am ever so grateful to my brother, Kourosh whose creative mind, determination and fortitude have been a perpetual source of inspiration. I also owe thanks to my wonderfully supportive friends, particularly Luis Pedro Nunes and Fausto Brito e Abreu.

As an academic researcher, my intention in writing this book was strictly to objectively describe and analyse a major indigenous social movement in Iran's contemporary history. I should add that any errors of judgement and fact are entirely my own.

INTRODUCTION

Seyyed Mohammad Khatami's election to the presidency in May 1997 signalled from the outset a period of immense change in Iranian politics. Khatami, one of the most enigmatic of modern leaders, was an important figure representing a powerful social movement in Iran. His reforms symbolised an effort to usher in an era of socio-political transformation predicated on a political platform that focused on consolidating the rule of law, encouraging political and intellectual discourse, stimulating civic activism and enhancing social liberties. Integral to this new path was Khatami's advocacy of an inclusive global discourse through his *Dialogue Among Civilisations* thesis, a kind of antidote to Samuel Huntington's more confrontational 'clash of civilisations'. Khatami's thesis, which advocated tolerance, peace and understanding, set the tone for Iran's rapprochement with the international community and internationalisation of the Iranian economy.

Yet Khatami's presidency produced an ambiguous outcome, leading many foreign analysts and much popular opinion in Iran to conclude that his reforms were ineffectual. While Khatami's reform strategy did have flaws, insofar as organisation, implementation and application were concerned, the largest impediment to reform was the character of the country's power structure. The political system in Iran is generally characterised by a multitude of loosely connected, generally competitive power centres, both formal and informal. The former are grounded in the constitution and in governmental regulations and take the form of state institutions. The latter include religious-political associations, martyr's foundations and paramilitary organisations aligned with various factions of the leadership. The president, as chief executive, is responsible for the everyday running of the country. He does not determine the general guidelines of Iranian domestic and foreign policy, nor does he control the armed forces or security apparatus. The political system, with myriad and overlapping centres of power with deep policy differences, frustrated Khatami's efforts to achieve substantive reform. As we shall explore, the legislative and judiciary branches had the power to obstruct – or to expedite – the implementation of Khatami's liberalisation measures. Owing to their staunchly traditionalist/conservative political orientation, these entities did not cooperate with the reform-orientated president. Any objective analysis of Khatami's achievements and shortcomings must consider these structural issues.

As we shall elaborate below, Khatami's small yet significant successes were largely overshadowed by an institutional gridlock that impeded many of his efforts to implement change. Between 1997 and 2005, reform efforts were stifled amidst intra-elite wrangling between conservative hardliners, who dominated the traditional economic and cultural sources of power, and the reform-orientated elements of society. Khatami was unable to manoeuvre around the political structure or to reconcile the political rifts that impeded his programme for change. Politically inexperienced in wheeling and dealing, Khatami espoused a vision that was extremely ambitious considering the constraints of the political office he held. More importantly, Khatami found it difficult to get across the message that he aimed to reform the system in order to *save* it. This would not have united conflicting camps, but it would have mitigated the tendency towards schism and factionalism. It can be argued that had he managed to deliver this message and to achieve broad-based political consensus, political evolution of the power structures would have been a naturally unfolding process.

All the same, burdened by a popular mandate demanding reform, and raised expectations, Khatami was accused of failing to live up to his campaign pledges. His second term continued to be marred by the confrontation between the factions, leading many of his supporters to become disillusioned and disengaged from the movement. The goal of this investigation is to unravel what really happened in Khatami's Iran, to provide a critical assessment of the period and to give credit where credit is due. In this study, we have tried to analyse in depth and at different levels, the ways in which normative and institutional components of reform fared in the context of the complexities of the Iranian power structure.

It is essential to keep in mind that the Khatami experiment, taken as a phenomenon, an institution or a movement, should not be measured against the standards of fully-burgeoned western, secular democracies. Rather, both Khatami's accomplishments and shortcomings must be judged according to the standards and constraints of the Islamic Republic of Iran – that is, in the context of a post-revolutionary and post-war society. Iran is a country whose geopolitical assets have been both a curse and a blessing. A country without strategic partners since the 1979 revolution, Iran has had to deal with the aftermath of a long and bloody Iraqi-imposed war (1981–9), diplomatic isolation and threats of containment and destabilisation. All of these factors served to harden the country's worldview by instilling in it a sense of insecurity and uncertainty.

Furthermore, the Iranian-Islamic revolution had produced a unique political system – a democratic theocracy. With no precedent in modern history, the Iranian political system was, and is, perpetually evolving. During this process of evolution, adaptation and change, the country has had to grapple with a host of day-to-day domestic socio-political issues, including economic challenges and demographic changes, as well as the need to function and integrate on a global level. It is important to bear in mind that Khatami attempted to implement his reform agenda in this particular context. Any objective analysis of the Khatami era needs to factor in the peculiarities of the country, as well as its historical setting, in order to provide a balanced picture of both the strengths and weaknesses of the reform project.

It is also useful to assess Khatami's presidency against the backdrop of Iran's past experiences with socio-political development. This historical background will allow us to determine the degree to which Khatami's political programme represented a continuation of earlier trends in Iran, or whether it signified a profound change. Traditionally, events in the early twentieth century have been taken to establish the long-term pattern of Iran's recent history. In the late 1920s and 1930s, Reza Shah Pahlavi, the army officer who first staged a British-backed coup in 1921 and went on to crown himself king in 1925, began fashioning an Iran based on a process of *tajaddod* – or renewal – and thus signalled an aspiration to modernise the country.[1] Political analyst Ali Ansari summarises Reza Shah's essence as being a 'modern version of the despots of old, harnessing all the tools and institutions of the modern age to his dynastic ambitions'.[2] Reza Shah established a pattern of forced modernisation that ruptured evolutionary patterns of development in the country. Iran was thrown back into authoritarianism, stunting the growth and development of inclusive government and popular representation. The Shah's ambivalent modernisation acutely lacked the spirit that characterises western progressive institutions and discourse, a spirit that derives from political openness and participation.

The Iranian Constitutional Revolution, spread over a period lasting from 1906 to 1911, was the first large-scale attempt to position the European idea of modernity within an Iranian social context. It introduced concepts of secularism and participatory politics into Iranian politics and political discourse. The key achievements of the constitution, modelled on the Belgian constitution, included the adoption of an independent judiciary (*edalatkhaneh*); the creation of a parliament (*Majles*); the granting of executive power to the cabinet, headed by a prime minister elected by the *Majles*; limitations on the absolute power of the autocratic monarch; and a bill of rights. Constitutional rule, however, was suspended under the autocracy of Reza Shah Pahlavi. The only choice thereafter was to try to westernise within the framework of autocratic government – a kind of 'modernisation from above'. The model survived for a couple of generations before its spectacular collapse in the 1979 revolution. The failure of Reza Shah, and later his son Mohammad Reza Shah Pahlavi, to modernise adequately fostered amongst the Iranian populace a backlash against the imposition of western-orientated culture. Increasingly, the masses attributed their economic and political grievances to westernisation, which they believed had fallen short of bringing prosperity and social justice to Iran. These ideas spawned a cultural movement that romanticised Iranian and Islamic traditions and resisted western-centred projects. The 1979 revolution was the climax of this trend. In the chaotic aftermath of this time, the father of the revolution, Ayatollah Ruhollah Khomeini, sought to transform Iran with an alternative version of modernity, in the form of an Islamic republic. This system implied a combination or blend of divine rule, theocracy and democracy, modelled on a theoretical construct that the west had not seen before. This socio-political form represented the antithesis of the Shah's developmental model.

It was with the legacy of 'modernisation from above' and 'theocratisation' that Khatami was forced to come to terms. As mentioned earlier, the Islamic Republic of Iran was in a state of flux; during the process of assuming its final shape, it went through a period when it needed meaningful public input to guide its course. In the mid-1990s, the country's population, across the board, was rapidly undergoing change, largely in response to the pressures of urbanisation, migration, economic integration, globalisation, cultural exchange and diffusion, and the technological revolution that was sweeping the world. When Khatami suddenly appeared on the scene in 1997 with his surprise landslide victory, it symbolised the desire for gradual change, for evolution and development of the existing system in line with the changing dynamics, rather than a radical shake-up of the system, or an uprooting revolution. In this manner, Khatami's political project represented a departure from earlier trends in Iran, regardless of whether or not it resulted in profound change.

Between 1997 and 2005, Iran saw evolutionary social changes that unfolded at a measured pace; however, this process neither imitated the west nor followed a rigid interpretation of the Islamic past. In fact, Khatami's rhetoric accommodated historical, local and national experience with an acknowledgment of the accomplishments of western civilisation. Indeed, the distinctiveness of Khatami's path to reform lay in his advocacy of gradual institutional reform within the existing template of a theocratic republic. Change was to be characterised by simultaneous engagement with the future as well as the past, and by concentration on the indigenous rather than the imported. Change was to come about not as the product of a classical 'revolution from above', but was rather to be derived from below, specifically, from civil society, market forces and society's response to globalisation. Thus 'Khatami's way' was to transcend the sharp turns and revolutionary breaks that have characterised so much of Iranian history.

The task Khatami had set for himself was not an easy one. Indeed, before Khatami, no one in the Islamic Republic of Iran had attempted to introduce sweeping reform. If the Iranian-Islamic revolution was comparable to turning around an oil tanker, reforming the Islamic Republic of Iran became like shifting a dock firmly anchored to the shore. Although the reform programme never bore full fruit, it energised Iran's debates, its administration, economy and international relations. It is precisely Khatami's impact on both the substance and style of Iranian politics that are explored in this book.

The intention here is to provide three separate strands of analysis. The first provides an overview of Khatami's personal development, with a brief account of his childhood and career. The second theme explores the intellectual context of Khatami's reforms. This section also frames Khatami's reform movement in the context of earlier attempts to master socio-political and economic transformation. Throughout this investigation, we shall examine the general question of the role of individuals and their ability to bring about socio-political change in the particular case of Khatami. We shall explore his leadership qualities, his attempts to advance democratic reforms within a conservative political structure and his relationship with the public. This section will describe the shape of the Iranian reform movement, the power structure, factional divisions and the way Khatami related to these elements. This focus allows us to examine the thinking and dilemmas behind Khatami's choices, and looks at how these issues worked in practice. The third strand focuses on policy issues and, above all, on social, political and foreign policy. In each area, there were fundamental choices to be made, with constitutional and institutional barriers to overcome. These choices reflected the democratic momentum in Iranian society at the time.

These three themes interact to describe a fascinating period of Iranian reform. There were no easy answers to fundamental questions concerning method and policy, and as a result, Khatami's decisions were characterised by a combination of strategic and tactical considerations. How these were interwoven in an unfolding historical context to both push and pull Iran into the twenty-first century is the focus of this analysis.

1

THE MAN BEHIND THE MOVEMENT

Early Life

Khatami's rise to power reflects one the most unusual political biographies of recent years. Brought up in the distant town of Ardakan, and having spent years tucked away in a religious seminary in Iran's religious hub of Qom, only slowly did his leadership ambitions and vision of a modernised Iran emerge. Attracted to the study of philosophy and theology, Khatami went on to win a place at the University of Isfahan. Years later, he accepted responsibility for managing the affairs of the Islamic Centre in Hamburg, Germany. Upon his return to Iran two years later, Khatami's rise to power was meteoric: he went from the status of mere Member of Parliament to that of Minister of Islamic Culture and Guidance, and then further up to become a senior adviser to President Ali Akbar Hashemi Rafsanjani and Head of the Iranian National Library. On 23 May 1997, Khatami won an unexpected landslide victory, and the monolithic Islamic republic – the stronghold of tradition and religious conservatism – was for the first time to be governed by a president who had pledged to forge a reformed and 'modern' Iran.

How did Khatami manage to become leader of the Islamic Republic of Iran's first reformist movement? Any worthwhile answer must take into account a fundamental developmental issue: how did Khatami's upbringing and education shape his vision of a modern Iran? This chapter will explore essential factors in his background; the next will examine the situations that he faced and the ideas that shaped his politics. This survey of the relevant terrain of issues and circumstances should allow the sketching of a rough answer to the question that greeted his emergence as the leader of Iran: *Who is this Mister Khatami?*

One of seven children (he has two brothers and four sisters), Khatami was born on 29 September 1944 in the southwest town of Ardakan in the central province of Yazd (known to locals as 'the pearl of the desert'). Ardakan is one of Iran's oldest towns with a history that predates the birth of Islam by more than 1,500 years. Situated on a desert plain, it is some 300 miles southeast of Tehran. Ardakan lies on the Silk Road, the ancient trading route linking Asia with the Middle East, and has a distinctly ancient flavour with houses built of mud bricks in a traditional desert style. The town remains strongly traditional: when the muezzin calls the midday prayer, shopkeepers retire and the town shuts down.[1]

As with many prominent religious families in Iran, the Khatamis came from a long line of clerics. The black turban worn by Khatami (as opposed to the white turban of most *Shi'i* mullahs) indicates that the paternal side of his family claim direct descent from Prophet Mohammad. His father was Ayatollah Ruhollah Khatami, a distinguished religious scholar, known for his piety as well as his rather progressive views. This status was reinforced by the fact that he was appointed leader of the Yazd Friday prayers by Ayatollah Khomeini, the leader of the 1979 revolution. Described as warm and sociable, Ayatollah Khatami gave regular religious lectures, but spoke enthusiastically about a wide variety of subjects. However, as a family acquaintance notes, he was also a good listener, preferring to keep silent about unfamiliar subjects.[2]

Khatami's father was tolerant, encouraging his children to read widely – poetry, novels, newspapers and even publications frowned upon by other clerics. The Khatami children were also allowed to listen to the radio freely. In the words of a childhood friend, 'in the house of Ayatollah Khatami democracy reigned supreme. The family read what they wanted and said what they wanted. In this capacity, this clerical household parted ways with the traditional clerical families'.[3]

Ayatollah Khatami's openness stamped young Mohammad Khatami's character. As Khatami put it in an interview, 'My greatest pride and honour is being the son of a man who was totally trusting, open-minded and knowledgeable. I was born under the tutelage of a saint whose efforts were first and foremost to bring up his children as free-thinking individuals according to the needs of the time and place'.[4] Father and son were of similar minds, and frequently engaged in long discussions relating to philosophical thought and enlightenment.[5] Khatami credits his father with imparting to him the importance of living humbly, being devout and thinking with an open mind.[6] Khatami's mother, Sakineh Ziai, was the daughter of an aristocratic landowner and was 15 when she married his father. In Khatami's words, his mother was a virtuous person who taught him the importance of living dutifully and morally. She was a doting mother, but was also firm with her children.[7]

The Khatami family lived in a spacious mud-coloured house with a stone terrace, built around a large courtyard with a fountain. They lived in relative comfort for a clerical family. In addition to this residence in the centre of town, they also owned a smaller summerhouse a few miles away. Khatami's younger sister Maryam, a schoolteacher in Yazd recalls: 'we had no restrictions on anything … we could spend as much as we wanted to'.[8] Still, the Khatami children were encouraged to be productive. These principles were decisive in shaping some rather distinguished careers. Khatami's brother Ali, for instance, having earned a masters' degree in industrial engineering while studying in New Jersey, became a successful businessman. He later served as his brother's chief of staff during his second presidential term. Khatami's higher profile brother, Mohammad Reza, who studied at the University of Tehran and at Guy's Hospital in London, became a surgeon specialising in renal disorders. He entered politics with his brother's landslide victory, becoming Deputy Minister of Health, and later Tehran's Member of Parliament in the Sixth *Majles* during which he served as Vice Speaker. He also served as the Secretary-General of *Jebheh-e Mosharekat-e Iran-e Islami* (the Islamic Iran Participation Front), Iran's largest reformist party, and took over as publisher of the party's daily newspaper, the *Mosharekat* ('Participation'). Mohammad Reza married Ayatollah Khomeini's granddaughter – Zahra Eshraqi – a women's rights activist.[9] Khatami's eldest sister, Fatemeh, a mother of six who was also a former local government adviser in women's affairs, was elected as the first representative of the people of Ardakan in the 1999 city council elections.[10]

A childhood playmate from Ardakan describes Khatami as a precocious and calm child. He explains that both he and the young Khatami would avoid the public square where all the other children used to hang out and ride their bikes. Instead, he explains, they preferred to venture through the winding roads of Ardakan.[11] The boy Mohammad Khatami talked about becoming a doctor, but his father wanted him to become a cleric. Khatami completed primary and secondary school in Ardakan, then in 1962, before actually receiving his secondary school diploma, Khatami commenced studies at the 'Hawzeh Elmiye' seminary in Qom (*Hawzeh* is a term used in *Shi'i* Islam to represent Islamic academies). At the same time, Khatami had a strong interest in philosophical and sociological discourse, keeping abreast of the latest intellectual debates. 'We pursued progressive subjects', explains Khatami's friend and colleague, two years his junior. 'He was so well-informed and such an astute learner that for one hour a week he offered free tutoring to fellow students'.[12] According to his colleague, Khatami lent his books to students and advised them on what publications to buy. Al-e Ahmad's at that time seminal *Gharbzadegi* (West-toxication) was one book of Khatami's that was frequently on loan.[13]

Recognising his son's interest in philosophy, Ayatollah Khatami sent the young Khatami to the University of Isfahan, where he completed a bachelor's degree in western philosophy. It was here that Khatami became exposed to western narratives of freedom and civic responsibility. Ironically, it was while reading philosophy at Isfahan that Khatami developed a revolutionary awareness, becoming influenced by the writings and teachings of Ayatollah Khomeini, at that time in exile in Iraq. Although he played a peripheral role in the revolution (he was abroad when it occurred), Khatami became a member of the Association of Muslim Students at the University of Isfahan, and helped prepare anti-government leaflets and bulletins against the policies of Mohammad Reza Shah – a huge risk given the ubiquity of the Shah's secret service, the 'SAVAK'.

In 1966, Khatami entered the University of Tehran where he obtained a masters' degree in educational science. Unlike most clerics, who typically avoided the military, Khatami fulfilled his two-year mandatory military training as a junior lieutenant in the Shah's army in Tehran. His sister, Fatemeh, justified this move: 'he [Khatami] looked at the military as an education he should have … it was not considered support for the Shah'.[14] In 1968, Khatami was offered a scholarship at a foreign university of his choice for an advanced degree, but he refused the offer. Instead, he returned to Qom to complete his previous studies in Islamic sciences. He studied there for seven years and completed the courses to the highest level.

In 1974, at the age of 31, Khatami married Zohreh Sadeqi, the daughter of a distinguished religious family. As was the custom in religious families, Khatami was introduced to his future wife by his family.[15] According to Mrs. Khatami, 'my father went and spoke to him and then he came to our house. I met him just once before we married. I do not remember how long our meeting was, but it was longer than 10 minutes. I fell in love at first sight'.[16] Two months later, they married. Khatami's marriage could only further his growing connection to the clerical world. Zohreh Sadeqi's mother was the daughter of Grand Ayatollah Hossein Agha Qomi, and sister of *Shi'i* leader Mousa Sadr. What is more, Mrs. Khatami is the aunt of Ahmad Khomeini's wife, Ayatollah Khomeini's son. Khatami's marriage produced three children – two daughters and one son: Leila, born in 1975, Nargues, born in 1981 and Emad, born in 1989.

Shortly before the eruption of the revolution, in 1978, Khatami went to Germany to replace Ayatollah Mohammad Beheshti as Head of the Islamic Centre in Hamburg. This was one of the oldest Iranian *Shi'i* centres in Europe, and one of the key centres for political and religious activity during Ayatollah Khomeini's exile. As head of the centre, Khatami organised Iranian students studying abroad, and wrote leaflets in opposition to the Shah, learning German along the way. The call to fill this position required a very specific candidate. The post had been held by some particularly prominent *Shi'i* clerics, including Ayatollah Hossein Boroujerdi, who would later become Iran's *marja-e taqlid* (the source of emulation), a role of supreme importance for *Shi'i* Muslims.[17] The candidate for the Hamburg post would have to possess the highest *Shi'i* credentials, an outstanding reputation in the community, strong skills in oratory and, most importantly, a charismatic personality. However, Khatami's colleagues felt that the Hamburg centre was too small for Khatami, and they tried to persuade him to stay in Qom. They argued that there were more opportunities for him in Qom. Khatami was not convinced, and accepted Beheshti's call to Europe, which he explained in just a few words: 'to reach this place, I had an overwhelming feeling that it was God's will and that it had nothing to do with whether it [the Hamburg centre] was too small or too big. I felt I had to relinquish Qom and to go to Hamburg in order to fulfil my duty of serving Muslims'.[18]

The Making of a Leader

After the overthrow of the Shah in 1979, Khatami returned to Iran and was elected to the *Majles.* Between 1980 and 1982, he represented his home district – the Ardakan and Meibod constituencies – during the premiership of Mirhossein Moussavi. In 1981, at the suggestion of Ayatollah Khomeini, he took charge of the *Kayhan* newspaper, but he eventually resigned.[19] During the Iraq-Iran War, which Khatami called 'the holy defence against Iraq', he undertook various responsibilities including serving as both Deputy and Head of the Joint Command of the Armed Forces, and as Chairman of the War Propaganda Headquarters.[20] This was a bittersweet experience for Khatami, who witnessed much of the suffering sustained by Iran's soldiers and civilians, and who – like most of Iran's leadership considered this an 'imposed war', which in reality served the interests of the west.

Between 1982 and 1986 (during the Iran-Iraq War), and later from 1989 to May 1992, Khatami held the post of Minister of Islamic Culture and Guidance, a ministry commonly referred to as *Ershad.* This was the institution responsible for propaganda and censorship. Yet, in this position, he eased restrictions on films, music, art and literature, which earned him a national reputation as a 'moderate'. Khatami worked hard and was obsessed with his work during this decade. His daughter Leila, the oldest of his three children, recalls his absence from family life: 'in comparison with other fathers I can say he never in his life had enough time to be with his children'.[21] In relaxing dogmatic barriers, Khatami was ahead of his time, introducing a hint of the cultural openness that he would officially inaugurate during his presidency. It is important to recognise that in the late eighties and early nineties, terms such as 'reform', 'enlightenment' and 'moderate' were not the buzzwords they would later become. For the first time in post-revolutionary Iran, a minister was demonstrating markedly tolerant tendencies, in one of the most conservative and sensitive ministries. *Ershad*, as the doorkeeper of the country's political and cultural probity, has always been an extremely influential institution in Iran's political hierarchy, and its officials have had a lasting impact on the overall policy orientation of the Islamic Republic.[22] *Ershad* is responsible for steering the media of books, press, art, cinema, advertisement and public relations in a direction that would serve a set of overarching Islamic principles. In the mission statement of the ministry, these principles included:

> Increasing goodness based on belief and piety, cultural independence and the immunisation of society from the influence of the other cultures; raising public knowledge in different fields; the prosperity of talents and creativity in society; spreading Islamic culture and art ... and the goals of the Islamic revolution, expanding cultural terms with others, specially Muslims and the poor.[23]

Indeed, this was a tall order, and Khatami's apparent flexibility was not taken lightly. In 1992, the overwhelmingly conservative *Majles* forced Khatami to resign. In a resignation letter, Khatami complained of threats, and called the 'creation of a superior culture' a 'weighty responsibility' that had become impossible for him. He appeared before the *Majles* to hand in his resignation on 23 May 1992. Five years later to the day, he would be elected president of Iran.[24]

The question of how Khatami would reawaken the cultural openness of the Ministry of Islamic Culture and Guidance during his presidency will be elaborated upon below. In 2000, a member of the conservative *Jamiyat Motalefeh Islami* (Islamic Coalition Society) inveighed against the policies of *Ershad* by asserting that 'a country like Saudi Arabia builds a mosque in Rome for the purpose of religious propaganda, while we give concerts. Does the number of religious books [in Iran] ever reach that of love stories?'[25] This backlash foreshadowed the strong conservative reaction that would constrain Khatami throughout his presidency.

In 1992, Khatami was appointed Director of the National Library of Iran and, for a time, faded from public view. He developed a keen interest in the early internet and wrote two books. In the first, *Bimeh Moj* ('Fear of Tides', 1992), he compares Islamic and western thought and explores ways in which the west offers something 'that is one of the basic needs of human beings: freedom'. He adds, 'because of this freedom, the west enjoys strong economic, political, military, scientific and technical power'. In *Az Donya beh Shahr, az Shar be Donya* ('From the World of the City to the City of the World', 1994), Khatami examines western philosophical and political thought.[26] During this period, he taught the fundamentals of philosophy at graduate level in the Department of Philosophy at the University of Tehran.

In 1996, Khatami was nominated as a member of the Supreme Cultural Revolution Council (SCRC). The SCRC (a substitute for the Centre for Cultural Revolution) was a conservative-dominated body based in Qom. It was established in 1980 in a decree by Ayatollah Khomeini and was responsible for planning the cultural policy of universities based on Islamic culture. The focus was on selecting professors and drafting academic courses in line with the goals of the 1979 revolution.[27] The group of seven council members, between 1980 and 1983, and then thirty-six members in 1999, was expected to compile all the cultural policies of the country.[28] As president, Khatami automatically became head of the council.

It is interesting that a former minister who had raised the ire of the conservative leadership for his permissiveness in the Ministry of Islamic Cultural and Guidance was invited to the council. What is even more striking is that Khatami was invited by the Supreme Leader, Ayatollah Ali Khamenei, whose role is to serve as the spiritual guide for the Islamic Republic. Therefore, Khatami's liberal tendencies were clearly not as antithetical to the political leadership as they appeared to be, and besides, the Islamic Republic has always seen them as a balanced coalition in which slow and subtle shifts often occur in order to maintain a degree of equilibrium. Khatami's appointment to the council was just such a shift.

2

THE IDEAS BEHIND REFORM

Khatami's vision for reform was always pragmatic and cautious. A break from the past would encompass the promotion of civil society, the rule of law, economic integration and gradual rapprochement with the international community. At the same time, however, Khatami's blueprint for change was guided by the overarching goal of preserving Iranian-Islamic culture and the gains of the 1979 revolution. During his 1997 and 2001 presidential campaigns, Khatami stressed that reforms would not clash with Islamic principles. His route to reform was always via a broader interpretation of Islamic texts in order to adapt Islamic principles to the exigencies of the day.

This chapter will explore the inspirations and references for Khatami's vision of modernity in Iran. What becomes clear is that in Khatami's Iran, modernity did not have a western core. While transformation entailed the development of many norms and practices typical of western societies, Khatami's purpose was not an attempt to westernise. It will be shown that in Iran's modern history there were two explicit efforts to westernise the country. In both cases, development was based on 'importing' western modernity, and in both cases, the country failed to adapt and the experiment resulted in social unrest. Under Khatami, the task of development involved the enhancement and enrichment of existing democratic practices and procedures. Later, it will be shown that Iran's political structure is an increasingly complex web of theocratic and democratic structures. Khatami attempted to sort out this tangled web by enhancing the pillars of civil society and the rule of law, while leaving the theocratic structure of the organisation intact.

For Khatami modernity had a different starting point in Iran, and so would have a different outcome from the west. Mainstream theories of modernisation depict modernity as an ideology grounded in European cultural experience. Khatami questioned the genealogy of modernity and argued against the assumption that it was necessary to pinpoint the origins of this social process. Modernity's trajectories are multiple, he held, with different social and moral effects. He emphasised that modernity is a social construct that produces its own reality.[1] In many ways, Khatami decentred the unilinear path of modernity by proposing a more historically sophisticated trajectory of social development.

The path to reform was complex and very much a product of Iran's past experiments in social reconstruction. Historically, the question of orientation has plagued Iran's developmental history, characterised by two polar opposites. At one end were the Pahlavi Shahs, who were principally devoted to 'catching up' with western societies through the project of westernisation; on the other was Ayatollah Khomeini, whose project of 'theocratisation' was based on the repudiation of many western norms and practices. Under Khatami, Iran reached a historical juncture where development required a more nuanced and integrative approach. Khatami was quick to realise that transformation was essential. He saw the need to open up political space, as well as the importance of internationalising the economy and of fostering global dialogue. International relations, trade and commerce, women, the youth, the press, culture and the arts, he believed, would collectively contribute to the efficiency of the state and the welfare of society. At the same time, Khatami did not intend to dismantle the theocracy. Rather, he wanted to breathe new life into it and to ensure its durability through a series of reforms that he suspected were long overdue.

The History of Development in Iran

In the twentieth century, Iran witnessed three fully-fledged modernisation campaigns: the first was Reza Shah's reconstruction drive, during which Iran achieved accelerated industrial growth.

While the country also experienced western-inspired social changes, the authoritarian institutions and practices of the past remained intact. Reza Shah's son, Mohammad Reza Shah, followed suit with his state-sponsored modernisation programme, Iran's second major modernisation project. Both Pahlavi Shahs adopted a brand of westernisation that lacked the critical spirit that distinguishes western modernity, and a distinctive pattern emerged of 'modernisation without modernity'. The third response to modernity was the establishment of an Islamic republic – the first large-scale attempt to build a society based on the rejection of western modernity with a revolution 'from above'. Through the practices and rhetoric of *Shi'i* revolutionary activism, Ayatollah Khomeini constructed a non-western, local or indigenous variety of modernity. All three responses to modernity diverged from the standards established in the west.

During these projects, society and state were thrust into a purposive, ideological, state-driven transformation. Under the *ancien régime*, the rapid and forced implementation of a peculiar brand of modernisation was witnessed, which cannot be easily typologised. Following the 1979 revolution, the first Islamic republic was established, founded on a new code of law. In retrospect, these modernisation projects were extraordinary experiments, without historical precedent. Khatami tried to move Iranian politics beyond these tumultuous times towards a regular politics. His reform movement represented the explicit project of a 'return to normalcy'.[2] In the context of Khatami's reform campaign, the politics of normalcy reflected the state of a country that had endured years of turbulent social and revolutionary change. The attempt to link up with the past, to restore the torn fabric of society, to draw on intellectual traditions and the cultural and religious values of the past, all reflected this post-traumatic pursuit of a usable past as the grounding for contemporary Iran. Khatami's pragmatic approach was rooted in the attempt to base Iran's politics in the repudiation of revolutionary politics. However, Khatami embraced the contributions of these extraordinary times, and he pushed for change through simultaneous engagement with the future as well as the past. As such, his movement gave enormous importance to the defining features of modernising societies (specifically, democratic practices and procedures).[3]

At the same time, Khatami was committed to reform and modernisation; however, he did not wish to alter the fundamental theocratic structure of the Islamic Republic. Indeed, his allegiance to the revolutionary ideals established by the leader of the 1979 revolution, Ayatollah Khomeini, was indisputable. Khatami made this position clear after becoming president. Addressing a gathering at Ayatollah Khomeini's grave, he made the following statement: 'We declare to the world that we will continue to tread along Imam Khomeini's path … We will persevere to do so'.[4] On the eve of the May 1997 presidential elections, Khatami declared, 'Imam Khomeini's notion of *velayat-e faqih* is the main pillar of the Islamic Republic. All citizens of the Islamic Republic have a practical commitment to *velayat-e faqih*. This means that all those who live under this system must abide by this principle and regulate their conduct within the framework of the constitution'.[5] In other words, any reform initiative was to take place strictly within the framework of the post-1979 Islamic theocracy.

Imperial Westernisation: Modernisation from Above

Reza Shah's development programme was the precursor to Mohammad Reza Shah's 'modernisation from above'. Modernisation was fast-paced, state-directed and limited to industrial-military development. Reform began with the build-up of the army and expansion of the country's military capabilities. In June 1925, the Shah persuaded the *Majles* to extend the conscription law. The result was a growth of the army from 40,000 to 127,000 in 1941. The five-fold increase in the military budget – an annual average of 33.5 per cent of the total revenue from 1921 to 1941 – allowed for the development of a small air force and a navy based in the Persian Gulf.[6]

The Shah overhauled the administrative system in order to simplify the country's cumbersome bureaucracy. Ten new ministries were created or reorganised, with 90,000 civil servants. Infrastructure projects were also initiated, with the number of roads multiplying throughout Iran for the rapid deployment of the armed forces. In 1925, there were about 200 miles of road; by 1938, this figure had multiplied to 14,000 miles. On 16 October 1927, Reza Shah initiated construction of the Trans-Iranian railway, linking the Caspian port of Bandar Shah with the Persian Gulf port of Bandar Shahpur, a distance of 866 miles. Two more developments in transport and communication are noteworthy. Starting in 1926, flights to and from the main cities were carried out by the German firm Junkers, whose regular routes covered 1,740 miles. In the late 1930s, the Iranian government took over the service and commenced regular flights to Baghdad. Furthermore, by 1935, telephone lines with a total length of over 6,200 miles connected the main towns.[7]

The Shah also worked to rid the country of foreign interference. The 'capitulatory rights' of the nineteenth century, which provided extrajudicial privileges for foreigners, were abolished.[8] In 1927, the customs administration was removed from Belgian control, and administration of the telegraph system was assumed from the Indo-European Telegraph Company. In 1930, the right to issue paper money was taken away from the British-owned Imperial Bank and granted to the National Bank of Iran (Bank Melli Iran). In addition, Reza Shah barred foreigners, particularly missionaries, from administering schools, owning land or travelling in the provinces without police consent. However, despite these measures, the Shah did not succeed in reducing the influence of the Anglo–Iranian Oil Company.

The state encouraged industrialisation by raising tariff rates, establishing government monopolies, financing industrial plants through the Ministry of Industries, extending low-interest loans to entrepreneurs, and exempting imports of machinery from customs duties for 20 years. Consequently, the number of industrial plants grew from 20 in 1925 to 346 by 1941.[9] The growth of industry gave birth to an industrial workforce – the number of wage earners employed in plants increased from 1,000 workers in 1921 to 50,000 in 1941. During the same period, the labour force in the oil industry grew from 20,000 to 31,000. Another 170,000 wage earners worked in railways, ports, small factories, fisheries, coalfields and construction.

Cognisant of widespread illiteracy and its implications for national prestige, Reza Shah initiated reform of the education system from 1925 to 1930.[10] As part of his campaign to rid the country of obscurantism, the Shah attempted to raise the status of women. Educational institutions, including the University of Tehran, opened their doors to both sexes. Cinemas, cafes and hotels were threatened with fines if they discriminated against women. There was a decline in the Muslim practice of polygamy and an increase in paid work for women. Nevertheless, women were yet to attain the right to vote and to stand for public election, and men continued to be recognised as the legal head of the family and were entitled to more favourable inheritance rights.

The Iranian land-tenure system was believed to have slowed down agricultural and rural development. As the largest landowner in the country, Reza Shah had a stake in preserving the land-tenure system. He sought an agrarian policy that was favourable to landlords as part of his approach of co-opting the upper classes, who he hoped would become his allies. In the early 1930s, the Shah passed legislation that transferred agricultural tax from the landlords to the peasant cultivators. Land taxes, on the other hand, were reduced to a miniscule sum: in 1939, they accounted for 0.25 per cent of the total tax revenue.[11] He also decreed that *kadkhodas* (village headmen) were to be appointed by the landlord, instead of being selected by the villagers. Conscription and taxes on sugar and tea were an added burden on the peasants – this was a period before oil revenues constituted a significant source of income, and before projects like the Trans-Iranian railroad were financed by tax revenues.[12]

In his campaign to give the country a modern veneer, Reza encouraged the use of European dress. Traditionally, social propriety had required male Iranians to wear a headdress, both outdoors and at indoor formal gatherings. This headdress varied from the religiously inspired turban and the skullcap, to the well-tailored sheepskin hat favoured by landowners and the political elite. Reza Shah viewed the entire variety of traditional headdress as a symbol of Iranian backwardness. As a result, a new hat was introduced, known as the Pahlavi hat, which closely resembled the French military cap. Every Iranian male was ordered to wear one. In the later years of his rule, the Shah decided that even the Pahlavi hat was not modern enough so he ordered the use of the western broad brimmed hat.[13]

Other sartorial measures issued by Reza Shah included an official edict in 1936 outlawing the veiling of women. The Shah perceived veiling as a primitive and fanatical practice that separated Iranian culture from that of the west. Veiled women were asked to shed the Islamic *chador* that covered them from head to toe. The irony was that whereas Reza Shah perceived the decree as a liberating force for women, it actually kept many women at home. Veiled women, especially those over 40 years of age, felt exposed without the *chador* that had draped them since pubescence. Some women, however, ignored the law and continued to cover themselves up with the *chador*. The decree caused uproar amongst traditional groups who believed that the Shah was forcing radical social change through authoritarian measures.

Indeed, equipped with a powerful military, security apparatus and bureaucracy, the Shah ruled with an iron hand. The *Majles* became a rubber stamp institution, deputies were stripped of parliamentary immunity, political parties were banned, trade unions were outlawed and independent newspapers were closed down.[14] The Shah was unforgiving when it came to recalcitrant bureaucrats and unruly tribal chiefs, who faced harsh disciplinary measures, including the death penalty. Akbar Davar, a Swiss-educated jurist, was assigned the task of reorganising the Ministry of Justice, with the goal of curtailing the influence of the *ulama* (Islamic clergy). Davar introduced modified versions of the French civil code and the Italian penal code, and Qur'anic (*sharia*) regulations regarding marriage, divorce and family were codified in a body of secular law. Davar also transferred the *ulama*'s notary responsibilities to secular attorneys. Moreover, state judges were given the power to decide which cases should be handled by religious or secular courts. Other regulations of this nature included the creation of state agencies, depriving the clergy of their control over the administration of civil services; the replacement of religious *maktabs* with modern schools; the 1939 law decreeing state appropriation of religious lands and foundations; and the prohibition of pious passion plays and public self-flagellation.[15]

In an effort to centralise the state and society, the Shah restricted or banned minorities from the right to educate their children in specialised schools. Literacy in Persian was deliberately increased in the newly established schools, while literacy in non-Persian languages, including Azeri, Arabic and Armenian, diminished as community schools and printing presses were closed down. The Shah also took an aggressive stand towards nomads. Having defeated the tribes, Reza sought to ensure their containment by extending army outposts into their regions, disarming their warriors, conscripting their youth, confiscating their land and restricting annual migrations.

Although Reza Shah never articulated a systematic blueprint for modernisation, his reforms were guided by the desire to create a modernised and independent Iran. Western-style clothing, the elevation of the status of women, the establishment of schools, modern industrial plants, communication networks and banks suggested that Iran was on the western path of modernity. On the other hand, the Shah revealed despotic features, with a firm grip on personal power through expansion of the army, the security apparatus and the bureaucracy. Intolerance, political suppression, cultural homogeneity and corruption were amongst the most backward features of a regime that, on the surface, appeared to be converging with the west.

In the 1960s and 1970s, Reza Shah's heir, Mohammad Reza Shah embarked on a similar programme of state-sponsored modernisation, based on the conviction that industrial and cultural proximity with the west would clear the way for Iran's passage to modernity. The Shah's vision of transforming Iran projected a clear benchmark – making Iran into the world's fifth industrial power by the year 2000. The Shah failed to implement reform evenly, limiting the endeavour to the expansion of industry, the military and infrastructure, while neglecting both civil society and the indigenous economy. This path contributed to widespread political discontent and socio-economic disparities, which in turn contributed to revolutionary conflict.

Autocratic modernisation was imposed almost entirely 'from above'. There was no consultation with the masses, and government bodies primarily played an administrative role. The

Shah had initially intended to make the drafting of the development programmes an inclusive process. This took the form of the Budget and Plan Organisation – a group of ministers and economists presided over by the Shah himself. However, once ministers began cautioning the Shah about the effects of ambitious over-spending and the limitations of Iran's absorptive capacity, they were marginalised.[16] In the traditional style of Iranian autocracy, decision-making remained entirely with the Shah, with his ministers and prime minister as little more than administrative chamberlains.

The principal focus of Pahlavi modernisation was build-up of the country's industrial capability – the agricultural sector, despite being a major artery of the Iranian economy, assumed secondary importance. Homa Katouzian explains that by channelling state funds to the urban sector, the Shah inadvertently 'let agriculture die a natural death'.[17] Emphasis on the urban sector, he argues, had damaging results: it led to agricultural stagnation, a widening of the rural–urban gulf, with increased peasant migration into towns and cities (leading to unemployment and housing shortages), and a domestic food deficit that the government exacerbated by injecting oil-dollars into the urban consumption of domestic products and imports.[18]

Mohammad Reza Shah did introduce a land reform package as part of programme known as the 'White Revolution'. This, however, was guided by political rather than socio-economic considerations. The Shah, in order, to counter the threat of a possible 'red' revolution, pre-emptively initiated a state-sponsored 'white' revolution. The White Revolution, furthermore, was designed to curtail the influence of the large landowners and clergy who had deemed the Shah's westernisation programme a threat to their own economic and political status. Roger Savory maintains, 'The Shah, on his own initiative, had decided to take action in order finally to break the power of the landowning class, which of course included members of the religious classes as well as lay persons'.[19] The most disruptive component of the land reform, however, was the abolition of all tenancies, especially charitable lands belonging to the clergy.[20]

The Shah also implemented policies that were perceived unfavourably by the bazaaris, the traditional merchant class. During his anti-profiteering campaign of 1975–6, which sought price stabilisation in the bazaar, the Shah sent thousands of agents into the markets to find merchants resisting government orders; approximately 10,000 merchants were imprisoned by the end of 1977. The sense of alienation was palpable in the swelling number of bankruptcies filed and the number of licenses lost by the merchants. Given the bazaar's links to countless networks and supply chains in both the middle and lower classes of Iranian society, the campaign strengthened the base of the opposition movement and sparked the revolutionary mobilisation of the bazaar itself.[21] Misagh Parsa's study of the 15 protest statements issued by merchants between January and December 1978 reveals that the bazaaris' main grievances were political violence and the despotic nature of the state, followed by government corruption, poverty, taxes and inflation.[22]

Aware of his growing unpopularity, the Shah became increasingly isolated, and began relying on repression to ensure political stability.[23] The *Majles* had little de facto power: deputies were screened closely by the political police and were then vetted by the Shah. The alarm was also raised internationally by such organisations as Amnesty International, the International Commission of Jurists, and the International League for Human Rights, which accused the Shah of violations of human rights.[24] Ironically, instead of promoting civil society, the Shah intensified political repression during his westernisation drive.

In view of these inherent contradictions, imperial modernisation can be conceptualised as the hybridisation of two incongruent tendencies: economic acceleration, on the one hand, and the continued political backwardness, on the other. It is helpful here to visualise Iranian modernisation as a double helix, where one strand represents western economic and military aspirations, and the other represents the archaic political institutions retained in the system. Intertwined, the strands perpetuated a permanent state of contradiction and social unrest.

The Shah's modernisation campaign marginalised various segments of society. The middle classes and the modern bourgeoisie – despite massive wealth accumulation – denounced the Shah's method of rule and called for freedom, an upgraded educational system, a rational civil service and political participation.[25] The landowners, the *ulama* and the bazaaris expressed contempt for the land reform, the anti-profiteering campaign, the preferential treatment of foreigners and measures to limit their economic or political influence. Lastly, the peasants, factory workers and migrant workers protested against the displacing effects of reforms and the higher cost of living.

The Shah's experiment with modernisation represents the leadership's difficulty in adapting diverse, traditional values and institutions to the developmental paradigm adopted from the west. Imperial modernisation represented a reaction to, and repudiation of backwardness and an effort to remedy the condition through westernisation. The Shah was plagued by a dilemma: he was too modern to be backward and too backward to be modern. This ambivalence manifested itself in the project of 'modernisation from above' – a paradoxical trajectory towards modernity that engendered a binary opposition: western-style development and progress, alongside classic eastern despotism. In effect, the autocrat-reformer, in so fashioning his conception of modernity, produced a hybrid that, little by little, brought the country closer to irreconcilable conflict.

Islamic Theocratisation: Revolution from Above

The failure to modernise effectively led the Iranian populace into an emotional backlash against the imposition of what they perceived as western-orientated culture. Increasingly, the masses blamed their economic and political grievances on the Shah's westernisation programme, which they felt had failed to deliver either prosperity or social justice to the country. These ideas spawned a cultural movement that romanticised Iranian and Islamic traditions and resisted western-centred projects. The Iranian-Islamic revolution and the system that followed can be interpreted as a revolt in defence of culture and tradition.[26] Reza Davari-Ardakani describes the revolution as a reaction to 'west-toxication', portending the end of western domination and the beginning of a new era in which religion would dampen the 'holocaust of west-toxication'.[27]

In 1979, Ayatollah Khomeini and his supporters overthrew Mohammad Reza Shah. The main tenets of the revolution were opposition to secularism, the promotion of a populist social-theocratic system, and opposition to the Great Satan – America – and its Israeli allies. This backlash was very much a response to the Shah's westernisation and secularisation campaign, which led to alienation of the non-westernised, more traditional segments of society. The Shah's US-backed, costly enterprise had intensified the Manichaean view of Ayatollah Khomeini and his followers of a world polarised into divine good and satanic evil – a worldview that helped the Iranian revolutionaries to cast the Shah and America as devious forces and to stir up action against them.[28] The popular 'revolution from below' against the Shah was quickly followed by a 'revolution from above', a state-sponsored project of transformation based on the return to an idealised Islamic past, and rejection of the western reading of modernity. The most notable feature of the post-revolutionary system was that, unlike in western societies, religion dictated the nature and structure of government and society.[29] This atavistic transformation, however, had a loud, eschatological resonance. The 1979 revolution was a critique of the present and a break from the past to a future-orientated utopia. The Islamic Republic of Iran was believed to be a springboard to a *Shi'i* utopia by virtue of its theological structures, institutions, laws and practices aimed at creating the conditions for the return of the *Mahdi*. Iran's *Shi'i* Muslims believed that Ali, Mohammad's son-in-law, was the rightful successor to the Prophet, followed by 11 other Imams. Twelver *Shi'ism*, the branch of Islam that has been Iran's official religion since 1501, holds that the twelfth Imam, the *Mahdi*, who disappeared in 873 AD and is thought to be not really deceased but in hiding, will one day return to bring justice to the world.[30] Ayatollah Khomeini's theory of Islamic government was based on the idea that instead of waiting for the return of the 'hidden' Imam, the leading *Shi'i* clerics should assume both clerical and judicial authority. The clerics were required to select one of their own as the Supreme Leader (*vali-e faqih*) whose essential qualifications were knowledge of *sharia* Islamic law (the basis for the country's legal system) and justice in its implementation. The November 1979 Iranian constitution laid the foundation for the *velayat-e faqih* (the rule of the Islamic Jurist) dating back to the *Shi'i* idea of waiting for the reappearance of the prophesied 'hidden Imam'. According to the Ayatollah, those in charge after Prophet Mohammad – the Imams – had been entrusted with interpreting Islamic codes, and with disseminating them among Muslims. In the absence of the Imams, the *vali-e faqih* was required to carry out these tasks. Although the power of the *vali-e faqih* was vaguely defined, in practice, the constitution invested the Supreme Leader with the final authority over all aspects of state affairs.

Other constitutional articles created new theocratic institutions, making Iran the modern world's only theocracy (these institutions are explained below). Ayatollah Khomeini became the supreme religious and political leader and the posts of president and prime minister became the second and third highest offices, respectively. Upon Khomeini's death in 1989, the constitution was amended. The post of prime minister was abolished and some executive powers were transferred to the presidency, creating an uncomfortable partnership between the elected president and the Supreme Leader. Since 1989, the president has appointed the government, though all ministers must be approved by the *Majles* (Islamic Consultative Assembly) before taking office. In addition to the *Majles*, however, the Iranian regime was made up of other powerful assemblies. Among these organisations, which are still functioning, are *Majles-e Khobregan* (Assembly of Experts), *Shura-ye Negahban* (Guardian Council) and *Majma-e Tashkhis-e Maslahat-e Nezam* (Expediency Discernment Council).

The Assembly of Experts is responsible for selecting both the country's spiritual source of emulation and the Supreme Leader. The body is comprised of 86 clerics who are popularly elected, though vetted by the Guardian Council. Its primary task is that of selecting the Supreme Leader and the members of the Guardian Council. The Assembly can theoretically dismiss the Supreme Leader if he fails to meet specific criteria or becomes unable to execute his duties satisfactorily. The Guardian Council, consisting of six theologians appointed by the Supreme Leader, and six jurists nominated by the judiciary and approved by the *Majles*, is responsible for approving all bills passed by the *Majles*, and for making sure they conform to the constitution and Islamic law. The

Council also has the power to veto candidates in elections to the *Majles*, local councils and the presidency.[31] The Expediency Council was set up in 1988 by Ayatollah Khomeini. Made up of 31 members appointed by the Supreme Leader, its role is to mediate disputes between the Guardian Council and the parliament. Since 1989, however, it has also advised the Supreme Leader on matters of national policy if the traditional methods have resulted in stalemate. In such cases, the Expediency Council is empowered to override both the constitution and *sharia* law in order to protect the interests of the state.

Having laid the institutional basis of Iran's theocracy, Ayatollah Khomeini proceeded to secure the foundations of administrative authority through a network of revolutionary forces and organisations. In 1979, he created the Islamic Revolutionary Guards Corps (IRGC), a political army defending the achievements of the revolution, which would act as a counterweight to the regular army still dominated by the monarchists. The most powerful paramilitary organisation in Iran after the IRGC is the *Basij*, a hard-line militia also assigned to safeguard the gains of the revolution.[32] The *Basij* was established by Ayatollah Khomeini's 1979 decree ordering the creation of the 'Army of 20 million' to protect the Islamic Republic against both American and domestic enemies. During the Iran-Iraq War, the *Basij* sent volunteers to the front.[33] In 1982, *Hizbullah* (literally, 'the party of God') took power into their own hands by confronting demonstrators, the offices of presses critical of the regime, and the premises of opposition organisations.[34]

In August 1982, the Supreme Judicial Council declared null all un-Islamic laws adopted since 1917. The Council also instructed judges to make decisions based on the Islamic codes and on the *fatwas* (Islamic edicts) issued by reputable clerics. Secular judges who presided over the courts in pre-revolutionary Iran were replaced by the *ulama*. All the major seminaries – as opposed to universities – became centres for the legal training of the *ulama*. Islamic revolutionary courts were introduced into civilian and military sectors that dealt with counter-revolutionary activity, and later with moral offences.[35]

Islamicisation also extended to the education system. In the summer 'Cultural Revolution' of 1980, Ayatollah Khomeini urged his followers to rid the universities of communists and atheists. Furthermore, new teaching codes were introduced; textbooks were revised to portray the clergy as defenders of justice; new courses in Arabic, the 1979 revolution and the history of Islam were introduced; and applicants to schools and universities had to have strong ideological convictions.

Ayatollah Khomeini also sought to 'remoralise' society by ridding it of popular western influences, which he believed undermined morality and proper social conduct. Alcohol was banned, as were bars and discos. Only traditional music was aired on state-controlled television and radio. Western films and music were outlawed. Veiling of all women was made compulsory. Women were barred from participating in international competitions that did not accommodate Islamic dress.[36] Society was segregated along gender lines: co-education was banned, except at universities, where rooms were segregated according to gender.[37] Post-revolutionary Iran mirrored an idealised seventh-century Medinan polity, all the way from political structure to cultural consumption, to everyday public social behaviour.

Principles of Islamic economics were also introduced. Immediately after the revolution, there was a wave of nationalisation of industry and banks; interest banking was abolished as a violation of strict Islamic principles. A large part of the economy and industrial capital stock was allotted to religious foundations known as *bonyad*. Later on, with the onset of war with Iraq, the economy was run once more according to market principles. According to Saeed Rahnema and Sohrab Behdad, 'the Islamic government, after much toing and froing, ended up following pre-revolutionary strategies and policies, and went even further than the Shah's regime in introducing an open-door policy. From full indiscriminate protection of all industries, the Islamic Republic moved to the other extreme of exposing them all to market mechanisms'.[38]

The prevailing idea behind pre-revolutionary modernisation was 'catching up with the west by becoming like the west'. Modernisation was premised on *convergence* with the west in the sense that the worldview adopted in principle, though not in practice, was borrowed from western societies. On the other hand, transformation under Ayatollah Khomeini was modelled on a distinctly non-western theoretical construct. The development design represented *divergence* from the prevailing western norms and standards: 'catching up with the west by becoming unlike the west'.[39] The argument here is that both imperial and post-revolutionary Iran resulted in 'alternative modernities' – either by accident or by design.[40]

Khatami visions for reform hinged on the belief that the developmental imagery and convictions of the past had been exhausted. Khatami did not seek to westernise, 'modernise from above', or attempt to construct an alternative modernity. Rather, he departed from these earlier models by advocating a path that this study characterises as 'modernisation from below'. This blueprint for change represented a break from the trajectories of the past and a shift towards a homespun variety of modernity cultivated 'from below'. Modernisation from below offered Iran a fresh path to a novel conception of modernity – what may be considered a 'third way' to a post-modernity. In this discussion, it must be noted that the emphasis is on Khatami's *vision*, rather than *programme* for reform. Khatami had a distinct vision as far as goal definition and policy orientation were involved; however, he fell short of producing a structured programme for change based on a well-defined political strategy and course of action. All the same, it is important to explore this vision as it represents a conceptual and methodological shift in the history of development in Iran.

Reform: Towards an Iranian 'Third Way'?

From state-sponsored westernisation, followed by the creation of a non-western modernity in the form of an Islamic theocracy, Iran's experiments with socio-economic transformation reveal a perplexing and often contradictory encounter with modernity. Khatami's approach to development, however, suggests that he believed that modernity was compatible with Iranian culture, and that western-inspired practices could be successfully woven into Iran's national, religious and historical tapestry. In fact, it can be argued that Khatami moved closer to resolving a recurring dilemma in Iranian history: what orientation should Iran follow in its political, socio-economic and cultural development? According to philosopher Mohammad Javad Faridzadeh, by forging a 'third way', known as *khateh seh* (literally, the 'third line'), Khatami reconciled questions of modernity with *sunna* (Islamic tradition).[41] Faridzadeh argues that this line allowed Khatami to gain victory over an 'Iranian schizophrenia'. This expression was originally coined by the sociologist Dariush Shayegan, who insisted that Iran had undergone the change from tradition to post-modernity without the mediation of modernity; and was thus experiencing a deep malaise. Shayegan argued that the solution was to open up Iran to the new multicultural world in which people would have to accept the diversity of perspectives, be open to new experiences and discard the idea of a homogenous culture.[42]

Khatami's political platform recognised the diverse and integrative forces of globalised politics and economics, as well as the pressures for more openness and social liberties. His challenge, however, was to reconcile these characteristically 'modern' or western-orientated reforms with the traditional establishment's deep-seated anxiety over the possibility of 'west-toxication'.[43] Khatami realised that his reforms would have to be introduced cautiously and at a measured pace. Furthermore, he realised the importance of pushing forwards with progressive reforms within the existing Islamic political, economic and social template. In fact, in doing so, it can be argued that he was clearing a path to a more indigenous expression of modernity, or what can be described as a more 'traditional' modernity. The chosen trajectory was an organic or domestic adaptation of the western form of modernity to local and traditional elements. Another feature of this developmental model is that it involved a staged modification of the status quo rather than its complete abandonment.

The strategy of 'modernisation from below' represented a clear antithesis to 'modernisation from above': The impetus for reform was derived from below (market forces, civil society, popular mobilisation) rather than from above, and reform was not introduced at a rapid, displacing speed as had been the transformations during the 'extraordinary' times. In one sense, 'modernisation from below' was a model in that it offered a preconceived approach to development; yet in another sense, this is misleading as it was really a *non-model* inasmuch as it was not based on a schematised blueprint. As indicated earlier, Khatami did not have a solid programme for change. While he advanced a very sophisticated and nuanced political vision, he fell short of delivering a robust political programme. All political ideas ultimately depend on being effectively communicated, and implemented with precision, efficiency and above all, political dexterity. Without a strategy, Khatami's vision failed to materialise the way he hoped it would, as did his chosen path to modernity. Khatami's greatest shortcoming was in the practical issues of political delivery; in other words, putting theory into practice.

However, the absence of a political strategy can be explained by the fact that such an ambitious political vision required an ongoing 'testing of the waters' in relation to government institutions and the political elite. How far could Khatami really go? Did he have enough political space to manoeuvre and did he possess the foresight to develop and advance a solid political programme? Given the political characteristics of the Islamic Republic of Iran, the answer would be more inclined toward the negative. It is likely that Khatami relied on a path that would evolve from the real needs of the masses at different political junctures. This discussion will now centre on precisely what those needs were and how they manifested in the political milieu.

In the 1990s, Iran saw the emergence of a unique set of political, social and economic issues. The population had doubled since the 1979 revolution, resources were dwindling and Iran was being steadily drawn into the tide of globalisation. Questions were being asked about how to define a value system to defend the next generation of the Iranian-Islamic revolution in a global world, about how to internationalise the Iranian economy, and about how to attend to social welfare issues. A major concern was the youth: educated, worldly and technologically adept, the country's population was overwhelming young. They wanted access to higher education, training and technology, job security, comfort and higher standards of living. Iran was experiencing the global culture of consumption and expectations were rising steadily. However, those material aspirations were accompanied by a change of mentality.

The youth, and indeed broad segments of society, aspired to have more control over their political destiny. As they became more educated, and consequently more politically aware, Iranians demonstrated a greater desire to play a role in the political process. However, the centralised political system seemed out of touch with the masses and this distance frustrated many of these aspirations. Economically troubled, and socially restless, this Iranian generation born after the revolution became known as the 'Third Force'.[44] Khatami responded to this emerging reality, promising Iran's youth increased economic opportunities, social justice, individual freedoms, political tolerance and greater rights, particularly for women. His decision to introduce these reforms was guided by a plethora of pressing and penetrating questions that dominated debate in the contemporary Iranian political scene. At the top of agenda were these key difficult issues:

(1) *Democracy*: Is there a civil society in Iran, and how can it be reconciled with the concept of *velayat-e faqih*? Is pluralism compatible with religiosity?
(2) *Islam and modernity*: Can modernity be re-configured? Are there non-western varieties of modernity? How can Islam be interpreted in terms of the principles of modernity?
(3) *Islam and the west*: Are secularism and westernisation the same? Is selective philosophical borrowing from the west possible?[45]

The important aspect was that Khatami and the reformist camp did not wish to do away with the Islamic Republic, but to make it more progressive and in tune with the needs of the people.[46] As we have indicated above, Khatami was a staunch supporter of the principles of the revolution, which he regarded as 'a great historical transformation'.[47] In Khatami's view, the challenge facing Iran was to overcome the crisis that accompanies the birth of a 'new civilisation'.[48] He perceived civilisation to be 'an answer to the curiosity of humans who never stop questioning their world'.[49] Civilisation emerges to address these perpetually evolving questions and needs: 'civilisations change and there is no such thing as an ultimate and eternal civilisation … with each question that is answered and each need that is fulfilled, humans are confronted with new questions and needs'.[50]

Khatami was unrestrained in his criticism of western politics, which, he argued, aims 'to govern all corners of the world and to dominate the theory and practice of international relations'.[51] However, he made a distinction between the west's politics and western civilisation as a whole. He argued that while western civilisation had important weaknesses, it also had important strengths. According to Khatami, the west has advocated the ideals of liberty and freedom, which are 'the most cherished values for humanity in all ages'.[52] He emphasised that the west had castigated the notion of authoritarian rule and 'freed humans from the shackles of many oppressive traditions'.[53]

In his book, *Mardom Salari* ('Popular Government'), Khatami underscored the importance of political pluralism, insisting that the destiny of the Muslim people of Iran should lie in their own hands. He advanced the notion of a 'religious democracy', explaining that Islamic concepts such as consultation, consensus, equality and allegiance reinforced the notion of political participation and the rule of law. In his book, Khatami gives priority to civil society, the rule of law and greater political freedom.[54] Bulent Aras has noted that while Khatami did not describe freedom as anti-religious, he nevertheless emphasised that institutions that fail to appreciate the importance of freedom are doomed.[55] Yet, Khatami was highly critical of Iranians who identified themselves as 'secular intellectuals', asserting that their movement 'is superficial and cut off from the people' who actually want a place for religion in their lives.[56] On the other hand, Khatami was also critical of the 'parochialism and repressive visions of dogmatic believers'.[57] Moreover, he contended that most religious laws should be open to evaluation in accordance with the needs of the particular civilisation.[58] Khatami defended his criticism of those who would impose censorship as a solution to divergent viewpoints and interpretations by citing Ayatollah Khomeini:

> In Islamic government there should always be room for revision. Our revolutionary system demands that various, even opposing viewpoints be allowed to surface. No one has the

> right to this. It is crucial that Islamic government can make policies that benefit Muslims. Unity in method and practice is essential. It is here that traditional leadership prevalent in our seminaries will not suffice.[59]

Khatami was careful to phrase his promises in the legitimating context of Ayatollah Khomeini's legacy. The fact that he was able to quote the father of the revolution's statement – 'our revolutionary system demands that various, even opposing viewpoints be allowed to surface', and that 'the government … can prevent any matter, whether religious or secular, if it is against the interests of Islam' – added to his practical everyday authority and blunted the impact of criticism from both conservative and secular extremes.[60]

Khatami's reform movement represents an important departure in Iranian developmental history. Khatami expected to chart a 'third way' to modernity by parting ways with the development strategies of his predecessors. He rejected the westernisation strategies of the imperial days but, at the same time, he disagreed with the explicit repudiation of western influences. Khatami tried to move away from the paradigms of the past, and instead adopted a more integrative approach to modernity. As will be elaborated below, this choice was a function of changing demographics, the pressures of globalisation and the civilisational aspirations of a society in flux. Khatami's political platform represented a middle ground where western-inspired reforms would be implemented within the framework of Iran's national, historical and cultural experience. In other words, a civilisational upgrade was to take place in the context of an Iranian and Islamic identity. As we shall see in the next chapter, this endeavour resonated with the Iranian people, who on 23 May 1997 gave Khatami a popular mandate to fulfil his electoral pledges.

3

THE KHATAMI WAY

Backdrop of the Reform Movement

In order to understand the popularity of Khatami's political platform and his subsequent electoral victory, it is necessary to contextualise his campaign within a broader sociological and political framework. It is necessary to look at the immediate historical backdrop to understand the trends that were developing in Iran. Economic practicalities of real life in a post-war, post-revolutionary society had set the country on the path of reconstruction and recovery. Ideology and revolutionary zeal had given way to pragmatism as the country tried to emerge from isolation and integrate into the world economy. Iran's demographics were changing rapidly: the population was growing; men and women were becoming more educated and upwardly mobile. Meanwhile, the domestic political scene was marred by deep divisions, with factions squabbling over the nature of the economy, ideological issues, and social and moral norms. The seeds were sown for the power struggle that would ensue after Khatami took his oath of office. It was a sensitive juncture in Iran's political history because not only was the country transforming at a rapid pace, it was also headed for an irrevocable transition. On 23 May 1997, the electorate decided the orientation of that transition.

Khatami's election marked the beginning of the third Islamic republic. Enthusiasm for the election must be understood in the context of the fundamental social changes of the first and second republics. The first republic was formed in the immediate aftermath of the 1979 revolution, and had at its core Ayatollah Khomeini's use of social mobilisation to unite the masses and guarantee the continuation of the state during the heady days of the Iran-Iraq conflict. The second republic began at the end of the Iran-Iraq War in 1989 and was principally guided by new economic realities and wider strategic considerations. The second republic is associated with Ali Akbar Hashemi Rafsanjani's eight-year presidency following Khomeini's death in July 1989.

The Need for Reform

During Khomeini's final year, the leadership expressed anxiety about the ideological organisation and long-term goals of the Islamic Republic. Rafsanjani took the first steps to putting post-war Iran on the path to economic recovery through two successive five-year plans aiming to repair war damage, improve infrastructure, and increase production and growth via private and foreign investment. A pragmatist, Rafsanjani was both a successful merchant and an influential cleric who recognised the importance of 'worldly' matters, as opposed to strictly religious or ideological considerations. The post-war economy perpetuated by the de facto command economy was in a shambles. For almost a decade, the government bureaucracy controlled domestic prices, imposed a wage ceiling, kept the exchange rate of foreign currencies artificially high, subjected imports to government distribution, demanded numerous licenses for the establishment of new industrial enterprises, prohibited foreign investment in Iran and provided food subsidies. These policies had contributed to stagnation, high unemployment and inflation.[1]

Rafsanjani understood that privatisation and increased foreign investment were the engines of growth and development, and he proposed a new course that became known as *Towse-eh.* He surrounded himself with technocrats willing to compromise on ideological zeal in order to establish demonstrable economic results. The second republic would encourage consumerism instead of austerity. Moreover, the export-orientated, anti-western approach that advocated autochthonous economic institutions was rejected. Rafsanjani and the pragmatic-minded technocrats that surrounded him now embraced a proactive open-door policy that sought to take Iran out of its economic isolation.

Nevertheless, Rafsanjani conveyed his progressive programme for post-war Iran cautiously. He cloaked his aspirations for the Iranian economy in classic revolutionary garb, arguing that the revolutionary mayhem was over and that the Islamic Republic was ready to enter a new 'Thermidor' phase. This phase (taken from the revolutionary theorist Crane Brinton) conceptualised the period of convalescence after the fever of revolution, auguring the end of the revolutionary era.[2] Rafsanjani maintained that the unchecked radicalism of either the conservative right or left could undermine the survival of the revolution. Between 1989 and 1992, Rafsanjani was too weak politically to be an independent force and understood that in order to push his agenda forwards he had to form a tactical alliance with the Supreme Leader, Ayatollah Khamenei. He needed the institutional support of the Supreme Leader's appointees, particularly members of the Guardian Council, who had to vet all laws passed in the *Majles*. In fact, shortly before his presidential victory, Rafsanjani orchestrated various constitutional amendments while he was Speaker of the *Majles*. The most important reform was scrapping the prime minister's job, and arrogating its powers to the presidency. At the same time, Khamenei's position was reinforced with the addition of the expression 'absolute' into his constitutional title.[3]

Progress in the post-war years was rapid. The Rafsanjani government was determined to show that the privation of the war years was over and ran up a $28 billion foreign debt (much of it short-term borrowing). Personal income rose 20 per cent in the first three years after the ceasefire.[4] Social indicators proved promising: infant mortality was cut in half, and consumption of staples such as meat, sugar and rice increased dramatically. In the area of foreign policy, Rafsanjani adopted a distinctively softer line. Following the Iraqi invasion of Kuwait in 1990, Rafsanjani resisted hard-line pressure to undercut American foreign policy and supported the American-led sanctions against Iraq.[5]

During Rafsanjani's second term, from 1993 to 1997, cracks began to show in the system. Factional divisions penetrated deeper and the alliance between president and Supreme Leader became precarious. As debate erupted over the powers of the *velayat-e faqih*, Khamenei moved closer to Speaker of the *Majles*, Ali Akbar Nateq-

Nouri. Rafsanjani was rendered politically impotent. Meanwhile, the *Majles* failed to pass any significant legislation between 1992 and 1996, becoming sidetracked in heated moral issues.[6] The state became mired in factional disputes, economic mismanagement and declining oil revenues. People's hopes for a better economy were dashed by high inflation, shrinking per capita income and the visible disparity of wealth. The privatisation of over a thousand public enterprises was begun in 1993 but was suspended a year later largely because of widespread scandals and corruption that had accompanied the sales of state enterprises with the privatisation programme. Massive imports and the rise of the short-term foreign debt reached unprecedented levels. The situation became worse when President Bill Clinton announced an economic embargo on Iran in May 1995. The Iran-Libya Sanctions Act in 1996 (denounced by the European Union as null and void) blocked the international community from making large investments, particularly in Iran's energy sector. Whereas some foreign companies did invest, oil production was insufficient to meet internal consumption or to pay off the foreign debt. What was becoming patently clear was that a period of fundamental reform was required in order to save the system.

Khatami had taken into consideration the prevailing economic and political climate when he decided to run for office on a reform agenda. He and his supporters had calculated that a presidential bid based on a reformist platform was a winning ticket, the breath of fresh air the ailing economy required in order to get back on track. As we shall discuss below, Khatami pledged to revitalise the economy through free market reforms and the encouragement of foreign investment through 'economic diplomacy' on the one hand, and his commitment to social justice and the equitable distribution of income on the other hand – a strategy with broad public appeal in the historical context we have described.

The two decades prior to the elections of 1997 witnessed profoundly staggering changes in the country's demographics. Between 1976 and 1996, the population nearly doubled, rising from 33.7 million to 60 million. In the decade between 1986 and 1996, Iran's urban population grew dramatically, from 15.9 million to 36.8 million. While in 1976 there had been only one city with more than a million residents, by 1996 there were five such cities and an additional four cities with populations of over 500,000 and fourteen more with populations of over 250,000.

At the same time, education levels had also increased: the literacy rate increased from 47.5 per cent in 1976 to 79.5 per cent in 1996. This change was particularly significant among women and rural dwellers: after 20 years, women's literacy had grown from 35.5 per cent to 74.2 per cent; in rural areas, the literacy rate had climbed from 30.5 per cent to 69.3 per cent – a 130 per cent increase. The number of university students in Iran also accelerated during this period, rising from approximately 150,000 to 1.22 million. These extraordinary changes are most vivid when juxtaposed against illiteracy rates. The ratio of illiterate people to degree holders was 12 times smaller in 1996 than it was in 1976.[7]

Following the 1979 revolution and with the onset of the Iran-Iraq War, the government began to encourage a high birth rate, which had produced a youth constituency that came of electoral age in the 1990s. Thus, for example, a person born in 1981, at the beginning of the war, was eligible to vote in the 1997 presidential elections. Approximately 60 per cent of the Iranian population in 1996 was under the age of 24. This generation of young men and women was highly educated and upwardly mobile – a constituency that by 1997 comprised 25 per cent of Iran's 67 million inhabitants.[8] Ambitious, cosmopolitan and culturally diverse, Iranian youth began to demand jobs and outlets for social expression. These demographics are crucial to bear in mind as they played an important role in Khatami's electoral victory. As we shall elaborate below, the youth was a powerful constituency that shaped the political milieu in which Khatami came to power.

There was also a cultural shift in the mentality of the elite. Abbas Abdi was a leading figure in Iran's reformist movement and founding member of the reformist party, the Islamic Iran Participation Front (IIPF). He reported that most of the ideological elite had reached the conclusion that one of the chief obstacles in the path of development was the power structure's independence from the people. The state's reliance on oil revenues, he asserted, created a rift between state and society. The time had come to foster unity instead, and this implied entitlement to citizenship, freedom of expression and the rule of law. This thesis manifested itself in a flourishing discourse on politics and sociology. Mahmoud Alinejad explains, 'almost two decades after the revolution, the quest for a distinct cultural identity produced a new socio-political movement which, although retaining the critical language of the revolution, incorporated a democratic rhetoric, and directed the critique within'.[9] The movement was buttressed by a burgeoning press: in March 1989, there were 112 periodicals in print; by 1992, the number of publications had grown to 437. Although fewer licences were granted after Khatami left his post as Minister of Islamic Culture and Guidance, his conservative successors did not succeed in halting the trend, and over 100 new periodicals were licensed each year. Abdi claims the wave of publications in this period had an entirely different character and function from those established earlier. In fact, he goes so far as to claim that the daily *Salam* played a critical role in the creation and triumph of the reform movement.[10] It is important to recognise that by the end of Rafsanjani's presidency, civil society had assumed a different form and character: it was slowly expanding and pushing for a broader political space. Khatami must have been very well aware of the political and social climate; his campaign advocating open political discourse and pluralism was tailor-made to respond to the needs of a budding democracy such as Iran was in 1997.

Ideology and Factionalism

Since the early days of the revolution, two overarching ideological positions have dominated the Iranian polity: the conservatives and the radicals. The staunch conservatives, or the 'traditional right', espoused a moderate non-revolutionary position on the nature of post-1979 Iranian society. This group supported the sanctity of private property, a minimalist state, a free market economy and strict implementation of the *sharia* in social and cultural life. While highly ideological and hawkish on foreign policy matters, this group opposed revolutionary internationalism. They were supported by the bazaaris, the traditional Iranian bourgeoisie, the clergy, members of the Qom seminary, and the more ideological segments of society. The opposing bloc – known as the 'radicals' or the 'leftists', for want of a better term – supported the cause of the poor and the downtrodden through the export of revolution; they promoted redistributive and egalitarian economic policies; and they supported moderate socio-cultural policies. Another faction that gradually emerged from this spectrum was the 'modern right'. This faction advocated a mixed economy, the nationalisation of domestic industries, state taxation and more progressive views in socio-cultural matters. The factions evident in the complex Iranian political landscape essentially grew out of these three distinctive ideological inclinations.

Since the 1979 revolution, the conservatives have organised themselves into the *Jame-eh ye Rouhaniyat-e Mobarez* (Society of Combatant Clergy, hereafter the Society), which acted as a nucleus alongside affiliated organisations such as the *Jamiyat-e Motalefeh-ye Islami* (Allied Islamic Society) and the *Jame-eh ye Modarresin-e Hawzeh-ye Elmiyeh-ye Qom* (Society of Qom Seminary Teachers). Until the 1997 presidential elections, the Society was considered the most powerful religious and political group in Iran, occupying the most influential positions in the government. This faction played a key role in the victory of the pro-Khomeini forces before and immediately after the revolution; they thus considered themselves the rightful administrators of the country. The core goals of the Society were to protect the ideological gains of the revolution, to propagate Islamic teachings and to strengthen religious institutions and mosques.

In its original form, the 28-member central council of the Society was made up of several clergymen from Tehran with strong revolutionary credentials. Among the original members of the council were Khamenei, Rafsanjani and Nateq-Nouri – the latter being Khatami's chief opponent in the presidential race of 1997. Over the years, however, membership in the Society changed and the more left-leaning members split from the group in 1988. This group, including Mehdi Karroubi, Mohammad Moussavi-Khoeiniha, Mahmud Doai, Mohammad Tavassoli, Mohammad Jamarani, Ayatollah Hassan Sane'i, Ayatollah Sadegh Khalkhali and Khatami, announced the creation of the *Majma-e Rouhaniyun-e Mobarez* (Association of Combatant Clerics, hereafter the Association).

In a statement in 1988, Khatami highlighted the difference between the religious conservatism of the right versus the populist-revolutionary orientation of the left: 'Members of the Society were split from the very beginning of the revolution. Now, we have no choice but to pronounce our opinions as the Association of Tehran, because some views are being ignored ... There have been differences of opinion among the membership of the Society regarding at least seventeen points'.[11] Khatami's statement demonstrates the growing heterogeneity, if not the very significant rift, that existed among the political factions in Iran. A decade later, these ideological differences would become a source of perpetual conflict as the future president struggled to implement his reform agenda.

While they had no written manifesto, the Association expressed its views in *Salam*, in addition to the short-lived publication *Bayan*. Along with the *Mojahedin-e Inqelabi-e Islami* (Crusaders of the Islamic Republic) and the left-wing student organisation, the *Daftar-e Tahkim-e Vahdat* (Office for Consolidating Unity), the Society formed the backbone of the left. This faction was sensitive to the gradual decline of revolutionary fervour in the country and toned down its rhetoric – so much so that it eventually formed an alliance with the modern right in the fifth parliamentary election in 1996.[12]

The First Presidential Bid

The *Kargozaran-e Sazandegi* (Executives of Construction), or the modern right faction, was made up of a group of moderate Rafsanjani-era technocrats who challenged the monopoly of the Society and declared support for economic reform. The faction was formed during the Fifth *Majles* election campaign and its members were senior aides of former president Rafsanjani.[13] Leading up to the election, the modern right proposed amending the constitution to allow Rafsanjani to run for a third term in office and thus ensure continuation of his programme of *Towse-eh*. The conservatives' vehement opposition to this transparent ploy led Rafsanjani to distance himself from, and thereby end, the dispute by stating that amending the constitution was not in the interest of the regime.[14]

For their part, the conservatives pushed for the candidacy of 54 year-old Nateq-Nouri. They were so certain about the victory of this powerful *Majles* Speaker that members began to suggest there was no need for a multi-candidate presidential race. This was particularly the position of the Society's 'satellites' – the *Jame-eh Islami-ye Mohandesin* (Society of Islamic Engineers) and the Allied Islamic Society. Their view was articulated by Assadollah Badamchian, who went so far as to suggest that the people of Iran were bound by religious duty to reach a consensus on a candidate and to avoid the need for competition.[15]

Despite the fanfare created by the conservatives about Nateq-Nouri's candidacy, the first faction to endorse a contender was the left. In July 1996, the *Majma-e ye Hizbullah* (Assembly of Hizbullah) in the Fifth *Majles* (1996–2000) and the Coalition of the Line of Imam (born out of the Organisation of Crusaders for the Islamic Revolution), which included the Council for Islamic University Teachers, the Office for Consolidating Unity, the Association of Women, and members of the Militant Clerics' Association, announced that in the coming election they would support the candidacy of former Prime Minister, Mirhossein Moussavi.[16] A day after the press reported Moussavi's candidacy, the pro-conservative daily, *Resaalat*, announced that the Allied Islamic Society and its associated organisation, *Tashakholha-ye Hamsu*, supported Nateq-Nouri's candidacy.[17] The fact that the two satellites made the announcement independently of the Society documents the growing divisiveness within the conservative camp. Indeed, for some time, they had been wrangling over the direction of the economy but they eventually settled on support for Nateq-Nouri.

In October 1996, the Association announced it was resuming political activities (they had ceased their activities nine months earlier), and that they would support Moussavi's bid for the presidency.[18] The decision was welcomed by the *Kargozaran* (led by its Secretary General, Tehran Mayor Gholamhossein Karbaschi) and its supporters in the private sector. As mentioned above, the modern right and the Islamic left had formed a de facto coalition in the *Majles* because their ideologies had begun to converge: the left toned down its revolutionary rhetoric, while the modern right declared support for increased state involvement in the economy. It was expected that on the basis of their shared interests they would support the same candidate.[19] However, in October 1996, Moussavi made the sudden announcement that he would withdraw from the run for the presidency, and provided no explanation for his decision.

The first reports of Khatami's candidacy came in the daily *Jomhuri-ye Islami* ('Islamic Republic'), which disclosed that there was talk in political circles about Khatami's entry into the presidential race.[20] Khatami was always reserved about his candidacy – saying maybe, then no, then yes. At times, he seemed quite reluctant to run despite the hype around him. Were his reservations the product of a lack confidence in himself or in the prevailing political climate? As we shall see, during his bid for a second presidential term, Khatami displayed the same ambiguity, refusing to confirm his candidacy until very close to the election date.[21] This made him appear somewhat apprehensive, an approach that was inconsistent with a man who espoused such an ambitious project of social engineering and transformation. In fact, by all accounts, Khatami's dramatic landslide victory came as a surprise to the candidate himself. It was almost as if Khatami had underestimated his own massive iconic appeal, as well as the appeal of his message of Islamic democracy. Where did this sense of apprehensiveness derive from? As we shall elaborate in subsequent chapters, even as president, Khatami did not possess the institutional might he needed to initiate substantive change in Iran. So perhaps Khatami had foresight; possibly, he had calculated that the office of chief executive was simply not enough to accomplish the colossal task of modernising Iran.

In fact, Khatami's insecurity only intensified in his second term as he fell into a political gridlock with the country's powerful conservative rivals. Khatami discovered that the country's conservative institutions outranked (and would frequently overrule) him, and that he did not possess the relevant institutional tools to implement reform. Another factor that bred insecurity was popular fatalism, which argued that even if Khatami did have the will to affect significant changes, the conservative elite would simply not allow him to succeed. The view was that Khatami would never gain the upper hand given the fundamental and unalterable realities of the theocracy.

In January 1997, Khatami officially announced his nomination. The leftist groups – the Crusaders of the Islamic Revolution, the Office for Consolidating Unity, and the Assembly of the Hizbullah of the Fifth *Majles* all declared support for Khatami. Prominent veterans of the revolution also backed Khatami, including Moussavi, Behzad Nabavi (an ideologue of the Islamic left), Abbas Abdi, Akbar Ganji (a one-time revolutionary activist turned reformist journalist), Saeed Hajjarian (former member of the Ministry of Information) and Mohsen Sazegara (a founding member of the Revolutionary Guard).[22] The *Kargozaran* and the Rafsanjanites, who did not have a candidate of their own, backed Khatami's bid. In fact, the *Kargozaran* provided financing for Khatami's campaign, while Rafsanjani used the powers of his office to call for free and fair elections. Similarly, the *Kargozaran* supporter, Mayor Karbaschi, used the political machine of the office for campaigning purposes. These supporters were instrumental in setting up and directing Khatami's nationwide campaign.[23]

Of the 238 people who ran for the election, the Guardian Council qualified only four candidates for the presidential race. These included: Mohammad Reyshari, Reza Zavarei, and the prime candidates, Khatami and Nateq-Nouri. Reyshari was a 51 year-old arch-conservative cleric and former Minister of Intelligence under Moussavi and creator of the Special Court for the Clergy. Zavarei was not a clergyman but was conservative in his political and social views. Zavarei, a 61 year-old Member of Parliament since 1981, and a former intelligence minister, served as judicial advisor among the six lawyers of the Guardian Council.[24]

Khatami was the candidate for a coalition of reformist segments of society that coalesced under the rubric of the rule of law and civil society. This translated into autonomous political and social space, individual and social freedom, and the promotion of a more tolerant and pluralistic order. Khatami upheld this basic creed as Minister of Islamic Culture and Guidance. However, Khatami attached as much importance to Muslim religion and morality as to the introduction of a pluralist system.[25] This synthesis comprised the cornerstone of Khatami's approach to Iran's political, economic social and cultural development. On the foreign policy front, Khatami and his supporters advocated a more moderate line, focusing on rapprochement, coexistence and mutual respect among nations.

From the outset, Khatami was aware that his relatively progressive views would generate opposition among the conservative establishment. In his own words, Khatami ran for the presidency in order 'to give my services and to express my views about the running of our society, which are incidentally, contrary to many existing views'.[26] In spite of this, Khatami continued to hone his liberal image. In a speech at Tehran's Sharif University, Khatami told students of his call for legalisation of political parties and the expression of 'differences of opinion'. He also made a tacit overture to the west: 'if good will is displayed toward the revolution ... the road for talks and understanding on the basis of any type of belief will be open to all'. Khatami believed that society was prepared for diverse political ideas and choices. When asked about the elections, Khatami asserted, 'This is the first time there will be a major competition in the presidential elections'. He added, 'in the past, because of the crises and sensitivities that existed, there was a consensus of views on the president'.[27]

Khatami's political platform was particularly appealing for the youth of Iran. Mindful of their grievances – the product of stifled ambitions and aspirations – Khatami emphasised the importance of harnessing the energy of youth as a force for the country, with the statement that 'youth is not an enigma but an asset'.[28] The umbrella student organisation, the Office for Consolidating Unity, helped organise young people for laborious, time-consuming canvassing purposes. Nateq-Nouri, on the other hand, enjoyed the endorsement of the Society, the religious establishment, the majority of *Majles* deputies and the bazaar merchants, as well as the implicit backing of the Supreme Leader.

Since the early days of the revolution, the majority of powerful pro-Khomeini conservative *ulama* (including Nateq-Nouri and Supreme Leader Khamenei) remained close to or at least sympathetic with the bazaaris and the Allied Islamic Society. This camp, scattered throughout the Iranian polity and in major political institutions such as the Islamic Revolution Party, the Revolutionary Council, the *Majles*, the Assembly of Experts and the Guardian Council, championed the all-encompassing power of the clergy in all walks of life, and defended an economic system favourable to the interests of the bazaaris. In fact, Nateq-Nouri believed that the *ulama* were the rightful administrators of the country, and justified this in the following statement: 'It was the clergy who masterminded the revolution, who deposed the Shah, who gave martyrs and saved the revolution from the likes of Bani Sadr' (Abolhassan Bani Sadr was the Islamic Republic's first president who clashed with Imam Khomeini).[29] Nateq-Nouri also found favour with the Supreme Leader by taking the authority of the ruling *faqihship* to new heights: 'During the occultations, the supreme leader enjoys the same rights and powers as those of imams, the prophets, and his wishes are the commands and duty for all'.[30]

Early in the campaign, Nateq-Nouri emerged as the front-runner and in most circles, his ascendancy to the executive was almost preordained. In fact, Iran's political machine had never been so blatant in its backing of a single candidate who espoused the same staunch conservative views. Nonetheless, Khatami's platform for political reform, tolerance and civil society was rapidly attracting many supporters, compelling the conservatives to tone down their rhetoric. For instance, addressing women's issues, Nateq-Nouri expressed a relatively moderate position: 'We must do something about our erroneous culture when it comes to women'.[31] During the campaign, speaking to an assembly of public education teachers in Tehran, Nateq-Nouri inveighed that it was not true that he would impose a full-length, one-piece chador as the official attire for women if he won the elections. In his words: 'Some people have compared us with the Taliban and quoted me as saying that if I become president, I will make the wearing of the chador compulsory. I categorically deny such misquotations and false allegations. In my opinion, although the chador is the most commendable form of *hijab* (Islamic attire for women), I hold that any form of dress covering the woman's body is sufficient'.[32]

The conservative candidate also defended the public education system as the main bulwark against cultural invasion. However, while approving the need for cultural exchanges, Nateq-Nouri counselled vigilance. Otherwise, 'the people will unintentionally put the yoke of cultural invasion on their own shoulders'. Asked whether secular tendencies had a real foothold in Iran, he argued that the Islamic Republic had suffered a secular assault during Bani Sadr's term of office but that the threat of liberalism had passed.[33]

The presidential campaign lasted only 12 days, and most candidates' access to the state media, including the television and radio networks, was restricted. Although Khatami had little airtime, he made up for it in the televised presidential debates where it became widely evident that Nateq-Nouri could not compete with Khatami's charisma. Khatami campaigned tirelessly. 'He was a populist candidate, he would get on a bus and kiss babies and shake hands', observes Elaine Sciolino. She adds, 'and he had such an extraordinary personality and such charm. It sounds sort of trite or superficial, but he's as charming as Bill Clinton … He charmed the people of Iran. He charmed them with his personality, with his good looks, and with his promises'.[34] Nateq-Nouri, however, appeared distant and unable to connect with the public. His seriousness made him appear wooden and he seemed out of touch with a rapidly changing Iran.

In a major election speech, Khatami used such expressions as 'social justice' and 'national solidarity', leading some conservatives to accuse him of attempting to secularise the country in the name of democracy and freedom.[35] Three nights later, on 13 May, Nateq-Nouri made his official presentation, which focused on the economy, the ills of inflation and the *velayat-e faqih*. On the morning of Nateq-Nouri's speech, in a patently aggressive slam, the conservative daily *Jomhuri-ye Islami* directly challenged Khatami's loyalty to the institution of the *velayat-e faqih*, claiming that in recent days he had 'openly questioned' it as a principle of government.[36] This focus on Khatami was an addition of fuel to the flame, inasmuch as the paper in an earlier editorial had already engaged in a broad smear of Nateq-Nouri's opponents, Khatami included, accusing them of 'opposing the *velayat-e faqih*'.[37]

The conservative attack on Khatami was nothing if not determined. Nateq-Nouri launched a kind of psychological warfare by focusing on the reasons for Khatami's resignation as Minister of Islamic Culture and Guidance in 1992. He alleged that the moderate candidate had been excessively tolerant, consenting to the dissemination of dangerous liberal and secular ideas. He also blamed Khatami for the proliferation of various other controversial publications dealing with prostitution, corruption, women and youth rights, and even publications on Freemasonry. The hard-line contender accused Khatami of siding with the liberals and opponents of the regime, and of questioning the ideological underpinnings of the Islamic Republic. He accused Khatami of associating with the 'west-toxicated', and of sympathising with eccentrics, actors and the 'rap generation'. Khatami countered these criticisms by urging people to recognise that Nateq-Nouri was plainly distorting his philosophy. He accused Nateq-Nouri of relying on the backing of the Supreme Leader, and then unfairly manipulating that fact to his advantage in a democratic campaign.[38] The daily *Salam*, which had been supporting Khatami's candidacy, complained of behind-the-scenes activities against their candidate by the hard-line Revolutionary Guards: 'Some high-ranking commanders of the Revolutionary Guards are interfering with the presidential campaigns, and have made statements against Khatami'.[39]

The leftist *Mojahedin-e Inqelabi-e Islami*, led by former Minister of Heavy Industries Behzad Nabavi, warned of alleged fraud in the elections by Nateq-Nouri's supporters and decried what it called the 'amazing move' by the Guardian Council to ban election monitors from polling stations. The monitors were seen as a guarantee against election fraud and were to include representatives of all four candidates. The group also complained of interference in the elections by the Revolutionary Guards and the *Basij* force commanders through their active support of Nateq-Nouri and the proliferation of leaflets defaming Khatami.[40] A Human Rights Watch Report alluded to the closure of newspapers and magazines by the government, and the intimidation of non-clerical groups and parties by vigilantes.[41] In fact, the *Ansar-e Hizbullah*, the vigilante group comprising members of the Basij militias or veterans of the Iran-Iraq War, closed down Khatami's campaign headquarters in Tehran. They made the case that Khatami's headquarters were in violation of election laws banning the use of state funds and facilities for political campaigns, since the building was owned by Tehran's municipality, which was headed by the capital's mayor, Karbaschi.[42]

The conservative challengers did have legitimate and realistic cause for concern. A month prior to the elections, an experimental public opinion poll conducted by *Salam* gave Khatami a resounding lead in the elections. The poll was conducted among students and professors at the Medical Sciences Department of Arak University. It gave Khatami 62.3 per cent of the vote, compared with only 17.9 per cent for Nateq-Nouri. Reyshari came in third place with close to nine per cent of the vote. The objectivity of the poll was clearly in doubt as *Salam* did not explain how it was conducted, and the paper appeared not to have used internationally recognised sampling techniques. All the same, the national newspaper published the poll forecasting Khatami's victory.[43]

Adding to Nateq-Nouri's woes was the surprise announcement by two important professors of the Qom religious school that their influential religious society would remain neutral in the elections and would not back Nateq-Nouri as expected. Jafar Karimi (while on pilgrimage to Mecca) told the *Kar va Kargar* ('Work and Worker') newspaper that the Society 'is not a political party to declare candidates for the presidential elections … We have come to the conclusion that it is better to remain neutral in the coming election. The prestige of our Society is more important than introducing someone as a candidate'.[44]

The moderates, similarly, experienced a major setback. In a stunning reversal for Khatami, the central council of the influential workers' organisation, *Khaneh Kargar* (Labour House), announced that it would not be supporting any particular candidate, despite its long-standing ties to Khatami's leftist supporters. The *Khaneh Kargar* extended its influence across the country among working people and traditional families. In the past, headed by Ali Reza Mohjub, the group had put its support behind leftists, including the Association; during the Fifth *Majles* elections, it had supported the pro-Rafsanjani bloc.[45]

The 23 May 1997 voter turnout topped 80 per cent, a figure not seen since the early years of the revolution.[46] Even allowing for some inflation of turnout statistics, anecdotal evidence indicates many people, after not having voted in previous elections (especially women, young people and members of the middle class), went to the polls.[47] The contrast is striking – 29 million people voting compared to just 16 million four years earlier. When just two-thirds of the votes were counted, it was clear that Khatami had won by a landslide. He was leading Nateq-Nouri by about 13 million votes to five million, with only six or seven million votes still uncounted. In total, about 69 per cent voted for Khatami (29 per cent voted for Nateq-Nouri), giving him and his reform agenda a resounding endorsement. In this crushing victory, Khatami garnered 22 million votes. Even in Qom, the centre of theological training in Iran and a conservative stronghold, 70 per cent of voters cast their ballots for Khatami.[48] Khamenei soon confirmed Khatami as the Islamic Republic of Iran's fifth president, and vowed cooperation upon his taking office (at the end of Rafsanjani's second term).[49] Khamenei simultaneously made the limits on Khatami's freedom of action very clear: 'The nation expects all measures taken for their prosperity and well-being to be within the framework of Islamic laws and regulations'. He also stated that while none of the candidates would fill Rafsanjani's shoes, he hoped that 'the future president will be a personality similar to him'.[50]

23 May 1997: A New Chapter in Iranian History

The day of the election was such an electrifying event for Khatami's supporters that they adopted the date, naming their respective causes the 'Second of Khordad Movement' (corresponding to 23 May). This ritualisation of the day meant different things to different people: to the youth, it corresponded with the 'Day of Youngsters and the Youth'; to females, it was the 'Day for the Social Activism of Women'; to politicians, it was the 'Day of Peace and Independence'; and to the poets and storywriters, it was the 'Day of Flowers and Smiles'.[51] The international community welcomed the victory of a more moderate and pragmatic contender: in the United States, President Bill Clinton reacted favourably, calling the election 'interesting' and 'hopeful'.[52]

Interpreting the significance of Khatami's victory, political analyst Ezatollah Fooladvand points to the fact that on the eve of the Second of Khordad, Iran had a weary post-revolutionary, post-war populace. He argues that accountability had deteriorated, that political decisions were made behind closed doors and that people were feeling increasingly helpless. Fooladvand explains that Khatami had diagnosed this malaise and was offering a remedy.[53] On the other hand, many social analysts believed that Khatami was a 'compromise candidate' and that the conservative establishment had offered him as a palliative with the aim of softening the image of the Islamic Republic and keeping the burgeoning youth at bay. To others, Khatami was elected merely by appearing to be associated less with the ruling establishment. Mohammad Reza Tajik maintains that Khatami was simply perceived as a lesser evil, as a challenger to the establishment.[54]

There is no question Khatami was cut from the same cloth as the ruling Islamic establishment. As stressed throughout this book, Khatami's family ties, his Islamic background and training, his ideological inclinations, his government service, his membership in the Association and his involvement in the revolution are all credentials and commitments that would lead many to believe that he was no different from the hard-line, conservative elements of society. Khatami was in fact a solid clerical establishment figure, evidenced by the simple fact that he was approved by the ultra-conservative Guardian Council and sworn in by the Supreme Leader. His presidential ambition was not to bring an end to the Islamic regime but to save it by cultivating its democratic aspects. However, Khatami diverged from the traditional establishment by espousing more progressive views; namely, the need for a civilisational upgrade in line with domestic demands and outside pressures of globalisation and economic internationalisation. Nevertheless, the fact that he was approved by the highest echelons of the ruling establishment is encouraging as it suggests that even the most conservative elements of the Iranian polity recognised the need for change. Whether they were wholly prepared for, or could even imagine, the full impact of those changes is another matter entirely. The plain fact is that at a crucial juncture in Iran's history the ruling establishment accepted that it was time for the evolution of the revolution.

The Second of Khordad Movement was the product of Khatami's election. Made up of the left, intellectuals, politicians, technocrats and progressive clergymen who advocated reform, the movement stood against the conservative right faction. As will be discussed below, the two sides would clash over ideological issues. The disposition of the two camps can be depicted as follows: Khatami's supporters upheld civil society and the rule of law, on the one hand; and conservatives defended a more absolutist *velayat-e faqih*, along with centralised Islamic institutions, on the other. The Second of Khordad Movement attacked the forces of conservatism for what they perceived as parochial and dogmatic sentiments that only impeded Iran's progress towards becoming a fully-fledged Islamic democracy. They believed that the conservatives espoused a far too rigid interpretation of Islam, and instead advocated a more liberal-populist interpretation. They hoped to respond to society's calls for the rule of law and pluralism – albeit, under the rubric of the constitution, *sharia* and Islamic religion. In fact, in order to underpin their movement, supporters closely investigated Islamic texts to find a reading of civil society that was in line with Islamic tradition. The movement enshrined the principle that Islam was an adaptable doctrine, rather than an immutable and static dogma. They believed that Islam had to be creatively extended to accommodate society's needs, and that it had to adapt the state to the forces of globalisation and economic integration.

Khatami responded to a popular mandate 'from below' becoming the vanguard of the Islamic Republic of Iran's first significant social movement. He set the country on a developmental trajectory – modernisation from below – a path that aimed to respond to calls for reform within the structure of the Islamic Republic. Khatami's proposed project for change represented an emergent paradigm that neither aspired to assimilate, nor distinguish itself from, the institutional designs of the west. In other words, the system was not hostile to western conventions, but it did not slavishly imitate them either. Here, the roots of a more home-grown, indigenous and popular adaptation to modernity can be identified.

4

FROM SLOGAN TO PRACTICE

The estrangement of Iran from the west over two decades after the revolution contributed to the notion that Iran would follow a special path to modernity. Religious and political isolation had further encouraged ideas about Iran's distinct developmental scenario. However, in these same post-revolutionary years, Iranian life was circumscribed as a result of accumulating tension between state and society, brought about by a growing population and mounting social discontent. It was increasingly evident and acknowledged that the trajectory Iran had demarcated for itself was now facing a very steep uphill climb. The dialectic between backwardness and modernisation had once again shown that there was no easy resolution of traditional woes as Iran confronted the task of establishing a viable pattern of development. Khatami's victory exposed the deep disparity between the appearance of Iran's ostensibly secure monolithic state and its actual vulnerabilities and dilemmas.

The conceptual and theoretical orientation that Iran would follow in its socio-economic development had bedevilled the post-revolutionary leadership, which was firmly committed to the Islamic line, but also cognisant of the broad social changes taking place in society. Khatami's view was that in the post-revolutionary Iranian polity, Islam should not be the state religion or an ideology of government alone but rather an inclusive religious, democratic, pluralistic force. He believed in the need for a more cosmopolitan Islam – the product of his conviction that Islam must be creatively extended in order to be responsive to the demands of modern life.

The 1979 revolution sought a return to an earlier Islamic civilisation: a golden age. As a religious thinker, Khatami was fiercely devoted to the revolution; however, he and other reformists believed that to yearn for this golden period was an anachronism and that in practical terms it could no longer meet the needs of the modern era. What was needed was a more progressive Islam for a modern Iran. Khatami sought to progressively reshape and adapt the perceptions of faith into a viable, modern approach to government and society.

At the same time, Khatami emphasised the importance of indigenisation. This aspect made Khatami's thesis appealing to Iranians, even to many conservatives, as it emphasised the cultural, historical and religious fabric of the country. In the following passage, Khatami expresses the importance of returning to indigenous roots in order to chart a home-grown path to modernity. He refers to the western experience leading to the Reformation of the 16th and 17th centuries. The passage is important as it underscores Khatami's belief that tradition and modernity are not contradictory or exclusive. Specifically, it exposes Khatami's belief that modernity can benefit from, and interact with, tradition – that is, the inherited and complex evolution of things cultural, religious social, conventional and institutional. Khatami clearly rejected the notion that modernity only manifests itself when tradition is superseded or supplanted;

> Dismantling aspects of tradition must be based on indigenous models, not imported and artificial. Indeed westerners at the dawn of modernity were awakened by delving deeply into their tradition. Thinkers revisited the artistic tradition of the Greeks and the social traditions of Rome. Religious believers retuned to what they considered to be the most authentic aspect of Christianity, and hence the Reformation. And these returns to tradition and reappraisals ushered in the new epoch.[1]

At the same time, the passage is telling as it reveals Khatami's rather flawed understanding of this particular period of western history. While Khatami aimed to provide context for his argument, he missed the mark. To assert that the Reformation traces its roots to the rediscovery of Greece and Rome is too simplistic. The Reformation did not stem from the west's rediscovery of Greco-Roman philosophy; its roots can be traced to Nicolaus Copernicus' scientific investigations and discoveries in the 1500s, and the culmination of centuries of venality, corruption and malpractice within the Catholic Church. Granted, Khatami was couching some rather bite-sized ideas in an historical framework, yet this was done at the expense of historical accuracy.

The passage, however, unambiguously exposed the fact that Khatami was not calling for a break with the past, or for a secular world that rejected a constructive role for religion. The challenge he believed was to create a balanced vision that incorporated the past without ignoring the complexities of modern existence. Yet to create the flexibility in theology meant to break the Iranian clergy's monopoly on religious interpretation, a right reserved for the ulama, who historically – especially in their *Shi'i* version – considered themselves to be the guardians of the community. Khatami's argument was that a single, infallible interpretation would not meet the demands of modern Iran. While the reformist president succeeded in getting this message across to the broader public audience, it also raised public expectations. The harsh reality was that the reformist discourse introduced by Khatami and other Muslim thinkers was anathema to the deeply entrenched conservative bodies of the establishment, who felt that reform would signify a betrayal of the ideals and principles of the Iranian-Islamic revolution. As Chapter 6 will show, any substantive move towards pluralism was quickly thwarted by conservatives who controlled key instruments of the state.

The fact was that under the post-revolutionary leadership what was gained in ideological consolidation was lost in civic activism and political development. Khatami and his supporters believed that this was the endemic conflict that lay at the heart of Iran's political culture. The weak role and performance of representative institutions, they believed, was one of the most 'backward' features of the Islamic Republic. Thus, strengthening the roots of popular representation became a priority for Khatami and his allies. Khatami did succeed in introducing small yet significant democratic initiatives by fostering an atmosphere of openness and civic activism. However, the uniqueness of Khatami's approach lay in its pronounced observance of Islamic codes of law and the post-1979 Iranian constitution.

In fact, Khatami's strategy for *eslahat* (reform) was premised on the notion that the state and its institutions would continue to be involved in the theological, doctrinal and legal affairs of the Iranian people. However, society would develop a stronger civic culture crucial to a healthy democracy. This would serve to bridge the conceptual gap that existed between society and the state – a state increasingly lacking in civic input. Khatami's civil society agenda was complemented with his efforts to put an end to Iran's international economic isolation. In the process of liberalising Iran, privatisation, trade liberalisation, the removal of monopolies, the promotion of foreign investment and a unified exchange rate became policy goals. Thus, as we shall see in this chapter, the reformist current aimed to usher in a critical transition in modern Iranian history. While social development can never be divided into neat categories, this embryonic political, social and economic transformation signalled a shift between tradition and modernity.

Institutionalising Change

Khatami sought to institutionalise a civil society buttressed by the rule of law. The first step towards achieving this goal was to assemble a cabinet of like-minded ministers and to gain approval for them in the conservative-dominated *Majles*. The president-elect was advised that he would face opposition in the *Majles* if he failed to accommodate their wishes in appointing key cabinet positions. *Salam*, a newspaper which had supported Khatami during the election campaign, warned that the conservative faction in the *Majles* was 'getting ready for a serious confrontation with the president-elect' over his cabinet choices.[2]

The choices of Khatami's 22-member cabinet reflected the alliance formed during the election between the reformists and pragmatists, or the modern right. Of the twenty-two members Khatami presented to the *Majles* for ratification, no fewer than seven had PhD's, eight were engineers and all three clerics had higher theological degrees.[3] The anticipated conservative opposition was fierce. Most of the criticism was aimed at undermining the proposed Minister of Islamic Culture and Guidance, Ataollah Mohajerani because of his liberal views and his earlier hints about the need to renew ties with the United States. His commitment to the *velayat-e faqih* had already been questioned by *Majles* deputies.[4] Remarkably, Khatami succeeded in gaining approval for all 22 nominees on 22 August 1997.

The backgrounds and ideological commitments of some appointments are particularly good indicators of the orientation the government was about to take. Ali Movahedi Savoji, a key supporter of *Majles* Speaker Nateq-Nouri, asserted at the outset that Khatami would have 'no problem' if he appointed cabinet members from all factions, but warned him to 'stage close negotiations with the *Majles*' on his cabinet choices. Savoji was emphatic in advising Khatami to retain Ali Akbar Velayati as Foreign Minister, because 'it would take at least four years for a new foreign minister to be in full authority of this ministry'.[5] In the end, however, Khatami ended up nominating the pragmatic Kamal Kharazi for the post. Kharazi had been architect of Iran's efforts to assist the United States in gaining the release of American hostages in Lebanon in the early 1990s, and had served as Iran's Permanent Representative Ambassador to the United Nations for eight years.[6]

The nominee for the Ministry of Intelligence (internal security) was conservative cleric and parliamentary deputy, Ghorban-Ali Dorri Najafabadi. His nomination was seen as an important concession for the conservative opponents in the *Majles*. Najafabadi was formerly Chairman of the Budget and Planning Committee of the *Majles*, and was therefore fully competent to understand and shape the details of the country's economic development plans.[7] Khatami hoped that his technical background would bring about a balance between the pragmatic and ideological aspects of the position.

Bijan Zanganeh, the nominee for the Ministry of Oil, was expected to bring new vitality to the ministry, which was rumoured to be under the influence of interest groups. Zanganeh was formerly Minister of the Construction Jihad, which oversaw numerous infrastructure projects. It was hoped he would put an end to interest group activity and promote greater cooperation between the Ministry of Oil and other ministries, particularly the Ministry of Foreign Affairs.

Rear Admiral Ali Shamkhani, nominee for the Ministry of Defence and Armed Forces Logistics, was formerly a commander in the Revolutionary Guards. Given his experience, it was believed that he would push for greater cooperation between the regular armed forces and the Revolutionary Guards, resulting in less duplication of effort. The nominee for the Ministry of Economic Affairs and Finance, Hossein Namazi, had held this position in the 1980s. With the nomination and the reappointment of Mohsen Nourbakhsh as Governor of the Central Bank, it was expected that Khatami would pursue many of the pragmatic economic policies of the former president, Rafsanjani.

However, it was Mohajerani's nomination for the Ministry of Islamic Culture and Guidance that clearly signalled the shift in the ideology of the new leadership. The nomination of this liberal-orientated cleric was evidence that Khatami was going to run his former ministry with the same open-mindedness he had espoused as minister. Mohajerani was in favour of a more tolerant form of Islam that promised to defend artistic, political and intellectual pluralism.[8] This new orientation of openness was reinforced by Khatami's nominee for the Ministry of Interior, Abdollah Nouri. Nouri had served as Minister of Interior under the former president, Hashemi Rafsanjani, and was a Member of Parliament. Khatami gave him his old portfolio back, despite fierce resistance from conservatives. Nouri was so outspoken in his advocacy of far-reaching reforms that he was impeached by the conservative-dominated *Majles* after only two years in office.[9] Khatami also lived up to his campaign promise to enhance the role of women in government. As will be discussed below, Khatami promoted a number of women to high public positions.

Democracy and Society

Khatami believed that basic social change in Iran – caused by the disparity between the forces of transformation and static social and political institutions – could be brought about through democratic initiatives. He did not believe Iran's problems could be solved by violent revolutionary change; rather, he supported fundamental social and economic change through peaceful means. Specifically, this translated into expanding citizens' participation in the political domain, and implementation of the rule of law as articulated in the constitution. Khatami outlined these principles in his inaugural speech at the *Majles* on 4 August 1997:

> Protecting the freedom of individuals and the rights of the nation, which constitute a fundamental obligation of the president upon taking the oath, a necessity deriving from the dignity of man in the divine religion … provision of the necessary conditions for the realisation of the constitutional liberties, strengthening and expanding the institutions of civil society … and preventing any violation of personal integrity, rights and legal liberties. The growth of legality, and the strengthening and consolidation of a society based on a legal framework for conduct, interactions and rights, will provide a favourable framework for the realisation of social needs and demands … In a society well acquainted with its rights and ruled by law, the rights and limits of citizens are recognised.[10]

Khatami further asserted that 'the overall policies of the Executive branch will be based on institutionalising the rule of law; vigorous pursuit of justice … promoting and consolidating the principle of accountability … [and] empowering the people in order to achieve and ensure an ever-increasing level of their discerning participation'.[11] The public was hopeful in waiting to see whether Mohajerani would introduce major reforms in the ministry or simply yield to pressures from the conservatives. Rather than toning down his views, Mohajerani embarked on some of the most progressive cultural policies ever enacted in the Islamic Republic. Following Khatami's lead, who held that 'guidance' in the ministry should not be translated into persecution, Mohajerani announced that the ministry was not out to ambush writers and artists.[12] He explicitly declared that no censorship or controlling of any kind would be imposed on printed material prior to publication. One wonders whether this shift from censorship to self-censorship was lost on Khatami.

The Ministry of Islamic Culture and Guidance liberally issued the required publishing permits for a string of dailies, periodicals and newsletters. This mild version of *glasnost* soon led to the mushrooming of an oppositional press and a vocal student movement. Print media were particularly vociferous, raising many issues that had previously been off-limits. Journalists, analysts and academics relentlessly called for public accountability, judicial impartiality and transparency, bureaucratic integrity and personal liberties. In particular, new newspapers such as *Jame-eh*, *Tus*, *Neshat*, *Khordad*, *Sobh-e Imruz*, and weeklies such as *Rah-e No* and *Aban*, together with *Salam*, *Iran-e Farda*, *Asr-e Mah* and *Kiyan* debated controversial religious, ideological and political topics once deemed sacrosanct dogma by the conservative establishment.

The print media's vibrancy could be seen in the host of new bookstores, newsstands and book exhibitions, which became popular with the public, particularly the youth. Anoushiravan Ehteshami commented that newspaper kiosks had become hubs of political discussion and debate, or what was commonly known as *gofteh-guh* (dialogue).[13] An educated and critical public emerged throughout the country with an appetite for reading diverse newspapers, journals and magazines. With the encouragement of Mohajerani and his deputy Ahmad Borgani, the first Assembly Guild for Writers and Journalists of the Press was established in December 1997. At the same time, with increased frequency, the Ministry of Interior issued permits for peaceful demonstrations and the formation of new political parties. Foreign observers saw the proliferation of the print media as a sign of loosening state control over the media and welcomed it. To many Iranians, these measures were all proof of the birth of a new public space in Iranian politics.

The Ministry of Islamic Culture and Guidance was also generous in issuing licenses for art exhibitions and cultural programmes. A collection of over 400 important paintings that had not been on display in Iran since the revolution had been stored in the vaults of the Museum of Contemporary Art. The museum's new director in 1998 obtained permission from the Ministry of Islamic Culture and Guidance to place the collection on regular display, reflecting Khatami's call for greater cultural openness.

Openness also signified greater official tolerance of social and cultural mores. Islamic dress codes for men and women were soon enforced less aggressively. Various sports arenas and gymnasia were opened to young women athletes and exercise enthusiasts. Private possession of western video cassettes and compact diskettes was officially permitted. Private parties were less frequently raided; internet cafes started popping up across Tehran; and satellite dishes were more and more evident on the rooftop landscape. Iranian filmmakers were allowed greater leeway in dealing with ideologically delicate subjects and film directors also succeeded in rebuking past governmental censorship by winning coveted prizes at international film festivals.[14] Under Khatami's movement the line dividing private and public space became more clearly drawn. The public domain – at least in the ideal sense – was not to infringe on the private, and people began developing a sense of greater self-worth and independence.

Women and Change in Gender Politics

The new reform government had to respond to the dual pressures of women's grassroots demands and expectations, as well as international calls for progress on gender equality. Khatami recognised the importance of this constituency's backing (about 40 per cent of the electorate who voted for Khatami were women), and frequently spoke about bringing women into the public sphere. Again, there was disparity between Khatami's real intentions and his ability to translate into policy measures. What was clear was his progressive position on gender issues – this is made evident through comparison of the first, second and third development plans.

The First Economic, Social, Cultural Development Plan of the Islamic Republic (1989–93) addressed female education and stated the following goals:

- Improving the condition of women through education and increasing women's participation in the socio-economic affairs of society and family.

- Bringing about a higher level of participation among women in social, cultural, educational and economic affairs, while maintaining the values of the family and the character of Muslim women.[15]

The *Second Development Plan (1994–8)* – which had already been issued when Khatami assumed the presidential office – briefly touched on the issue of female education by stating the following as a goal: 'Paying attention to the education of girls and the literacy training of women and young mothers'.[16] The 2001 *National Report on Women's Status in the Islamic Republic of Iran*, published by the Centre for Women's Participation (*Markaz Mosharekat Zanan*), clarified the female education priorities of the period covered by the *Third Development Plan (1999–2003)*. This document reflected the concerns of its time and demonstrated a deep transformation in the approach to gender and education. It viewed education as a woman's basic human right and called for increased gender sensitivity in all aspects of schooling. The report specified the following as the priorities of female education:

- Revising existing education laws that are gender biased.
- Reducing gender gaps in the fields of science, mathematics and applied sciences.
- Modifying educational materials in order to portray the correct image of women's roles in the family and society, and of the mutual rights of women, men and the family at all levels.
- Emphasising the participation of female specialists in planning and policy making at all levels of education.
- Developing and promoting counselling services in high schools to prepare and guide students towards more appropriate fields of study in order to eliminate the concentration of female university students in certain degrees.

- Determining a particular quota for creating equal opportunities for women in a number of specific university degrees.
- Teaching management skills to women with the aim of enhancing their participation in the sphere of decision-making.
- Expanding and diversifying technical and vocational training programmes for women with a view to creating employment opportunities.[17]

The most tangible measure undertaken by the Ministry of Education to reduce gender bias in schools was the revision of certain textbook pictures during 2002–03 in order to portray more girls engaged in traditionally 'male-orientated' tasks, especially in the technical-vocational fields.[18] The shift in language in the period covered by the *Third Development Plan (1999–2003)*, and the approach undertaken regarding the question of gender, was a reflection of the changes in Iranian society since the onset of the reform movement in 1997. These changes included: the active and visible role of women in the 1997 presidential elections that led to the victory of the reformists and the election of President Khatami; the presence of a few articulate female representatives in the parliament, elected in 2000, who pursued women's rights in the public and private spheres; the viewpoint of Khatami himself regarding the rule of meritocracy regardless of gender; the active role of newly established centres for women's studies at different universities, female-orientated NGOs and Women's Bureaus at various ministries promoting women's rights; and increased relations with international organisations. Although the reformists were criticised for their inability or unwillingness to address sensitive gender issues and to introduce radical change, such as their failure to appoint a female minister, they were relatively successful in raising public consciousness and advocating the need for gender sensitivity in all spheres.

There are some clear cases to be cited in relation to the issue of gender. For instance, Khatami appointed Masoumeh Ebtekar as vice president of environment and women's issues, and Zahra Shojai as his adviser. Shojai became head of his coordination body on women and the Centre for Women's Participation. Later in 2001, Khatami nominated Zahra Rahnavard as his senior adviser on cultural affairs. The judiciary, the legislature and the executive each had special institutions set up to advise them on women's issues. The percentage of seats held by women during the four parliamentary terms increased from just two per cent in the Third *Majles* (1988–91), to five per cent in the Sixth *Majles* (2000–03). However, it declined slightly in the first year of the Seventh *Majles* (2004).[19] Nevertheless, no progressive laws were passed on women's rights without women deputies having initiated them.[20]

In 1999, the percentage of females attending university surpassed the number of men for the first time since the revolution. The admission rate for females was about four per cent higher than for male students.[21] A woman was appointed as university president of Zahra University. In 1999, no less than 15 journals were devoted to women's issues. In unprecedented numbers women were involved in competitive and recreational sport. In 2000, Faezeh Hashemi Rafsanjani (the daughter of former president, Hashemi Rafsanjani), stated in an Iranian newspaper that about two million women participated in some form of sport, compared with only 400,000 in 1998, and 10,000 before the revolution. She affirmed that the breakthroughs reflected freedoms gained with the election of Khatami.[22]

At the end of Khatami's second presidential term, Farideh Ghayrat, lawyer and the representative for the Association for the Defence of Prisoners Rights, credited Khatami with creating an environment that encouraged women to participate in social life, although she still wanted to see more significant changes in the legal arena. Marzieh Mortazi-Langarudi, a reformist women's rights activist, told Radio Farda that female activism had been on the rise during the Khatami presidency. She added that women had increased confidence to fight for their rights. She observed that the religious norms tying a woman's fate to her gender and physique were challenged under Khatami's presidency. The following statement describes the key social trends that developed during Khatami's leadership:

> In general, the women's movement grew relatively well during the reformists' [leadership]. I think women's most urgent claim has been equality in human rights and gender rights. Steps have been taken. Women have more self-confidence in seeking their rights. I think that during [the presidency of] Khatami, there was no stagnation. Stagnation was before Khatami when no one could challenge the laws that appeared holy.[23]

In May 2005, Khatami's spokesperson, Abdullah Ramazanzadeh, defended the president's efforts at a meeting of deputy governors and governors-general for women's affairs: 'We had not claimed that we would be able to bring about sexual justice'. He added, 'nobody should expect us to bring about that kind of sexual justice in a matter of ten or fifteen years. What Khatami's government did was to turn the issue of sexual justice into an issue of the day, rather than allowing it to be confined to intellectual circles, to the extent that today no politician can easily ignore the issue'.[24]

Overall, Khatami's approach to gender issues is best interpreted as cautiously active. There is always the question of whether Khatami genuinely sought to incorporate women into the political process. While there is much evidence supporting his commitment to elevating women's legal-social status, participation of women in the public arena was more complicated. During Khatami's presidency, there was no specific action plan for creating opportunities for women in the political realm. However, considering the socio-cultural features of the polity and the country's traditional political mentality on gender issues, it is clear that even if Khatami sought to alter women's social status, he would encounter major obstacles. These obstacles included: internal disputes and factional rivalry, which overshadowed the question of gender; the extreme sensitivity of addressing women's legal rights since the latter fall into the realm of Islamic jurisprudence; the difficulty of transforming the patriarchal structure of a male-dominated society; and the absence of independent women's movements and truly non-governmental organisations that could challenge the status quo and initiate a grassroots movement to promote women's rights. While female activists continue to influence the society indirectly and implicitly through their professions, the only lawful voice heard belongs to 'Islamic feminists' within the ruling group. The latter are, for the most part, found in the parliament, where they have endeavoured to improve women's lives by seeking to reform laws that pertain to their public and private lives, including divorce, child custody, housing, inheritance, employment, retirement, domestic violence and reproductive health laws, all within the framework of the Islamic legal system. These women have worked actively to convince the ruling elite to accede to the United Nations Convention for the Elimination of All Forms of Discrimination against Women, while respecting the principles of Islam.[25]

Raising awareness of the contentious subject of women's rights was thus something that had to be done tactfully. Khatami's government responded to conservative pressure by addressing gender roles in the state structure in ways that did not challenge the dominant policy of gender segregation. Thus, for instance, Khatami's approach to women's advancement included the setting up of separate women's units in almost all government departments and executive agencies.[26] What is significant is that while the advances made in gender issues were relatively small, they were still unprecedented in post-revolutionary Iranian society. By voting for Khatami, women had established themselves as a founding force present at the dawning of a new civil society. In a patriarchal society that had been traditionally dominated by elder statesmen, the reality of women bringing presidents, parliaments and councils into power proved to be a shock. This wake-up call was the emergence of reformism in Iran.

Legislature Change: Local Councils and the *Majles*

The government was rewarded by citizens for its policy of freedom of expression when reformists attempted to extend their power base in the legislature. The reformers won the elections of both the local councils and the Sixth *Majles*, despite a huge process of resistance and obstacle-creation by the conservatives.[27] In February 1999, Khatami delivered on his campaign promise to hold Iran's first local elections in an effort to dispense power beyond the centre, as was originally mandated by the constitution. At a single stroke, 200,000 democratically elected officials entered the country's political structure, despite conservative parliamentarians' frantic efforts to block the candidacy of reformist candidates. It now became perfectly clear that in a relatively open electoral game the reform movement would continue to win hands-down.[28]

The Khatami government, through the Ministry of Interior, encouraged women to participate actively in the elections for the local councils, both as voters and as candidates. The Deputy Minister for Political Affairs, the key official for managing the elections, issued guidelines to local authorities urging them to encourage women to participate as candidates. Officials of the Women's Bureau of the Ministry of Interior organised and promoted across Iran more than 100 workshops and seminars to encourage the participation of women. To mobilise women, an advocacy non-governmental organisation, the Association for Women's Political Participation, was created.[29] Were these genuine steps to encourage female participation in the public arena? Or were these measures based on political calculation, specifically, that women, as a numerically powerful constituency, would back reformists over conservatives? The initiatives probably derived from both, considering Khatami's mentality, his position on gender matters, his political acumen and his awareness of local demographics.

The first elections to the city and rural councils took place in February 1999. About 25 million Iranians cast their votes to elect 236,138 representatives from among 328,862 male and 7,276 female candidates.[30] The reformists secured control of virtually every major city and most towns. The municipal elections were the first time Iranians elected local representatives. These elections were the reformists' first aggressive move towards decentralisation of power. They were thus both an exercise in the development of civil society *and* an implementation of the rule of law – the foundation of Khatami's reform movement. This initiative was probably one of Khatami's most unambiguous successes during his presidency.

The second attempt to consolidate the notion of Islamic democracy and popular government were the elections for the Sixth *Majles*. Approximately 69 per cent of the electorate turned out for the February 2000 parliamentary elections and chose a predominantly reformist – 215 out of 290 members – legislature. The Second of Khordad Movement represented some 20 parties and organisations, including: the Executives for Construction and the Party of Moderation and Development, both considered more pragmatic or centrist groups; the IIPF; the Islamic Iran Solidarity Party; the Islamic Labour Party; the Association of Combatant Clerics; the Mojahedin of the Islamic Revolution Organisation; and the Office for Consolidating Unity. In total, the pro-Khatami candidates won over 60 per cent of the seats. In the key constituency of Tehran, the reformists took almost 30 seats, and most seats in a host of other towns and cities.[31]

Reformist candidates sometimes replaced generally popular candidates who had allied themselves too closely with the centrist list that had supported Rafsanjani. The problem for the technocratic centrist camp was the close association of its leader Rafsanjani with the conservatives. This association led the electorate to marginalise the centrist front, even where specific members had had close and long-standing ties with the leaders of the Second of Khordad Movement. Another relevant observation regarding this election is that remarkably few clerics entered the Sixth *Majles*. After a monopoly in the *Majles*, they saw their numbers shrink from over 150 in the First and Second *Majles*, in the early and mid-1980s, to fewer than half a dozen in the early twenty-first century. The clerics' growing disappearance from such an important institution as the legislature was symptomatic of a quickly evolving political landscape in an avowedly Islamic state. More telling is that the elections for the Sixth *Majles* indicated that Iranians fully grasped the usefulness of tactical voting, taking great care to ensure that their preferred spokespersons were elected. Consequently, many deputies were becoming representative mouthpieces of the public's desire to see change in the country's political, social and cultural atmosphere. The seed of this bottom-up transference of people's everyday concerns and troubles into legislative provisos and agendas was now planted.

It is also significant that before Khatami's investiture in 1997, only 39 parties, political societies and associations received permits from the 'Article 10 Commission' of the Ministry of Interior. The commission was comprised of representatives of the state prosecutor general, the political judicial council, the Ministry of Interior and two *Majles* deputies with the responsibility of issuing operational permits for parties, and supervising them. By January 2000, the number had increased to 103. Thus, just 28 months into the Khatami presidency, 64 new parties and groups had been granted operational permits. However, the fact remains that despite this notable increase the number of genuinely active and influential political parties and groups in Iran barely exceeded a dozen: *Jame-eh ye Rouhaniyat-e Mobarez*, *Jamiyat-e Motalefeh-ye Islami*, *Majma-e Rouhaniyun-e Mobarez*, *Jebheh-e Mosharekat-e Iran-e Islami*, *Kargozaran-e Sazandegi* and *Mojahedin-e Inqelabi-e Islami* were among the more significant.[32] Mohammad Reza Khatami was leader of Iran's largest political party, the *Jebheh-e Mosharekat-e Iran-e Islami*, which had 250 domestic party offices.

In February 2004, Mohammad Reza Khatami reacted to the conservative victory of the Seventh *Majles*, addressing the problems facing his party:

> In a country such as ours, where democratic tradition is still fragile, it is hard for parties to reach the public in the way that has become common in western countries. However, we will pursue our political objectives against all obstacles, and will use novel methods and tactics. It is very crucial for us to be an effective party in the 2005 presidential elections. Although we have lost these [parliamentary] elections, I believe we can get back to power within four or, at the most, eight years.[33]

The emergence of diverse political parties and groups in Iran during Khatami's leadership (albeit with restricted activities) is significant, as it reflected the evolution of civil society and democratic momentum 'from below'. Indeed, this was one of the most significant contributions of Khatami's project. The pluralistic momentum 'from below' continued to prevail under the conservative leadership of President Mahmoud Ahmadinejad. It manifests itself in a socially conscious and politically aware public that engenders a new Iranian sense of citizenship. Later we will discuss how Iranians continue to exert their will through the ballot box, demonstrating that the modernisation of Iran can indeed be achieved 'from below'.

The Politics of Economic Reform

Khatami had been elected on a platform of social justice. While many anticipated political reform, such as the development of pluralism and civil society, many were equally anxious for economic reform. Khatami did not inherit a healthy economy: inflation was high, unemployment was growing, particularly among the youth, and there was a vast disparity in wealth distribution. Investment and privatisation had yet to take off, and the economy was marred by poor management and a lack of funds for projects due to plummeting oil prices. In fact, the entire economy was faring badly and the costs of political and economic isolation over the years were becoming patently clear. *Forbes* magazine reported in July 2003, that 'with 9 per cent of the world's oil and 15 per cent of its natural gas, Iran should be a very rich country. It has a young, educated population and a long tradition of international commerce. But per capita income today is 7 per cent below what it was before the revolution and Iranian economists estimate capital flight (to Dubai in particular) at up to $3 billion a year'. The report blamed the state of the Iranian economy on economic mismanagement.[34]

Khatami believed that for the economy to grow it needed to diversify, decentralise and, eventually, privatise. For these ideas and schemes to come to fruition, a legal framework needed to be established. Khatami routinely blamed the country's 'sick economic structure' as the fundamental flaw in the economy. He was acutely aware that substantive economic development could not be achieved in the absence of an overall political strategy. He realised that investment-orientated economic development required a sound and secure environment that would attract potential investors. Normalisation of relations with the outside world was thus crucial (Chapter 5 examines Khatami's efforts to bring Iran out of isolation through diplomatic engagement with the European Union, Russia, China, India and other growing economies in the east). In order for Iran to make an effective transition from tradition to modernity, the dynamics of economic relations had to change.

In his economic address to the nation in August 1998, Khatami gave his verdict on the Iranian economy. He outlined his views on the economy, the fundamental problems of unemployment and job creation, inflation, the red tape of bureaucracy and his blueprint for restructuring. He underscored the need to manage government resources more efficiently, and to reduce and eliminate monopolies. He highlighted the need to cultivate a tax culture, to encourage the private sector and to foster greater competition among banks. He also argued that the government would provide mechanisms that would allow foreign currency to be held in Iran on which interest would be paid according to international rates. Other highlights of Khatami's economic plan included broad-based administrative and legal reforms pertaining to (1) the operation of businesses; (2) industrial laws governing such matters as deregulation and privatisation; and (3) the protection of civil liberties and increased transparency in government.[35]

Khatami delayed announcing his economic programme until the fall of 1998, when he submitted the 1999 budget to the parliament. His statement to parliament was more like a literary essay on social alienation and political empowerment than a budget presentation. The problem was that Khatami was trapped between the divergent economic views of his allies. His economic program has been an eclectic composition of the views of the two opposing factions. As discussed earlier, Khatami came to power in an alliance with two previously opposing factions: the modern right, encompassing the liberal coalition promoting economic liberalism, and the modern left, comprising the die-hard remnants of the populist-statist tendency that dominated Iran in the first decade after the revolution. Thus, on the one hand, he stressed that economic recovery required the mobilisation of domestic capital and increased foreign investment. In agreement with free-market advocates, Khatami declared that more investment was only possible if the state eliminated its control over the market. On the other hand, to appease his allies on the left and to maintain his mass appeal, Khatami pledged his commitment to social justice and the equitable distribution of income.

Khatami's main economic objective during his presidency was to reverse Iran's isolation within the global political economy. The subjects of privatisation and foreign investment were politically explosive issues within the traditional institutions of power. Numerous monopolies in Iran's economy were owned or controlled by the ruling elite who represented an alliance between the commercial bazaar bourgeoisie and conservative clerics. This powerful commercial entity supported the status quo and resisted giving up its economic privileges. Nonetheless, Khatami backed a five-year plan for 2000-2005, much of which was devoted to promoting the rule of law, non-oil exports, privatisation, and deregulation. Steps were taken to tax the untaxed, reduce dependence on oil, and further liberalise exchange rates and to bring them in line with international market rates (a unified single exchange rate was achieved in 2002).

In the end, relatively little was achieved, as most reforms would weaken the ruling clerics and their allied bazaaris who continued to have preferential access to credit, foreign exchange, and licenses and contracts, which made it difficult for others to compete. Strict limits of foreign investment, a weak legal framework, the dearth of productive investment by the bazaar bourgeoisie and corruption created obstacles to economic reform and development. There was some economic recovery, including a build-up of industries, and increased manufactured products under customs protection. However, Iran still did have export markets for industrial products. The economy remained overwhelmingly dependent on government-controlled oil income, and per capita GDP remained lower than pre-revolutionary levels despite some increase. Iran still had low wages and high unemployment even amongst the educated. Faced with the needs and support of the poor, Khatami turned away from neo-liberalism in some areas, refusing to privatise various public services and retaining subsidies on necessities. He also raised the wages of public employees, some of whom, like teachers, were paid below the official poverty level.

Over time, there emerged a consensus about the importance of foreign trade and investment. A chain of progressive legislation aimed at liberalisation was enacted, including legislation ensuring that Iran would be treated fairly in the international economy. This series of laws included the Law on International Commercial Arbitration; the Law on Accession to the New York Convention on Recognition and Enforcement of Foreign Arbitral Awards; and the Amendment of the Tax Laws. Two important acts of legislation stand out: first, the Law on the Attraction and Protection of Foreign Investment (LAPFI), which broadened the guarantees for foreign investment, as well as easing the bureaucratic procedures for registration and protection. Second was the expansion of this law in the Foreign Investment Promotion and Protection Act (FIPPA) in 2002.[36]

To stimulate foreign trade, the government removed non-tariff barriers and streamlined export regulations by removing export taxes and levies. The establishment of tax-free zones with incentives and exemptions helped to boost foreign interest in the country. New rules were also introduced allowing foreign investors to invest on the Tehran Stock Exchange. Khatami also announced plans for a new oil trading market that would compete with the London International Petroleum Exchange. Khatami's greatest contribution to Iran's economy was the active 'economic diplomacy' he engaged in, in an effort to improve Iran's image and to secure trade, loan and investment agreements, though constitutional provisions on foreign investment continued to limit such investments.

This chapter has described how Khatami and his allies attempted to reform the country in the face of increased popular appeals for participation in the country's social, political and economic development. By emphasising the democratic rather than theocratic aspects of the constitution, Khatami took steps to execute the reformist goals of developing democratic institutions and pluralism. These policy objectives were translated into action. As we detailed above, the first step was to assemble a cabinet of pragmatic ministers that favoured the reformist agenda. For instance, a tolerant Ministry of Islamic Culture and Guidance was elected, which was largely responsible for contributing to the emergence of a lively press and vigorous public debate, breaking many taboos of the Islamic revolutionary tradition. At no other time in modern Iranian history had the country witnessed such a surge in cultural and artistic activity. The policy of openness was put into practice in the – albeit cautious – advocacy of women's rights. Popular representation was further put into practice with the creation of the municipal councils, which served as a vehicle for public expression. Now the public had a chance to define the ideals and direction of the Islamic Republic through free and active participation at the ballot box. The composition of the 1999 local councils and the Sixth *Majles* was dramatic evidence of popular enthusiasm for the reform movement.

Khatami's civil society agenda was complemented with some small steps to liberalise the Iranian economy. Iran's political isolation meant that there was significantly less foreign investment in Iran than in the rest of the region. Khatami's economic policies reflected a commitment to creating a new favourable climate for foreign investment. However, this flurry of democratic initiatives had the effect of raising public expectations by creating the impression that Iran was genuinely witnessing the birth of the 'religious democracy' that he had routinely mentioned in his speeches. When Khatami's reform efforts were met with systematic resistance from the conservatives, those expectations were met with disappointment. Consequently, many of Khatami's supporters began to grow impatient, blaming him for failing to orchestrate a sustained campaign for the cultural and social freedoms they desired. As will be discussed, the conservative reaction was so severe that it undermined much of Khatami's authority and credibility. Frustrated, many supporters accused Khatami of failing to seize the moment, while many international observers perceived these setbacks as predictable, convinced that the reformist president was a mere palliative, nominated to soften the Islamic Republic's image, and that he never had any genuine intention to implement substantive change.

As we shall see, Khatami soon found himself in a precarious position vis-à-vis his conservative rivals; increasingly, he began to focus on ensuring his own political survival. He thus eventually became more of a spokesman rather than leader of the reformist movement. We mentioned earlier that Khatami had entered the upper echelons of Iran's political arena with some reluctance. Given his apprehension and what seemed to be a lack of genuine conviction in his ability to reform the system considering the idiosyncrasies of the political machinery, it was not surprising that Khatami showed reluctance to 'rock the boat' because it could result in his own political demise. The Supreme Leader was perhaps correct when, exasperated by 'illusions fostered abroad', he explained that Iran was not the Soviet Union and that Khatami was not its Gorbachev.[37] The next chapter will examine where these 'illusions' came from, in describing Khatami's success in improving Iran's international image by dismantling the wall of isolation that had been built around it.

5

KHATAMI AND THE WORLD

Unveiling Iran's Iron Curtain: Dialogue Among Civilisations

Globalisation has led to a questioning of how people can live in a world that is so interconnected, involving close contact, yet not sufficiently dialogical to confront in an efficient way the inter-cultural conflicts, disagreements and differences. Khatami's background in philosophy led him to explore and examine the specific features and problems of a globalising society, with a particular focus on the self and identity issues. The notions of self and identity reflect the deeper regions of the zeitgeist in a developing global society.[1] Khatami, reflecting this zeitgeist in the discourse of the *Dialogue Among Civilisations*, effectively challenged the then widely held theory of the inevitable future clashes between cultures. The philosophical underpinnings of this thesis are elucidated in Khatami's statement:

> Effective engagement in a dialogue among civilisations and across cultures requires an understanding of essential concepts and relationships. One of the most basic of these is the relationship between dialogue and knowledge. Knowledge is the product of dialogue and exchange: *speaking* and *listening*. Once complemented by *seeing*, they constitute the most important physical, mental, and spiritual faculties and activities of human beings. Seeing expands the realm of knowing; it strengthens and solidifies the self. One talks to others and listens to others, but seeing is realised from the vantage point of the *self* and the world, and humans become the subject

> matter of the self. Speaking and listening, on the other hand, are efforts by two or more parties aimed at coming closer to truth and achieving understanding … The concept of the dialogue among civilisations and cultures is based on such a definition of truth, and is not in conflict with philosophical definitions of truth. Nor is it principally about speaking. In effective dialogue among civilisations, listening is as important as speaking.[2]

Philosophy has a rich tradition of dialogue from Plato onwards, and the thinking and rethinking of self and identity in the light of classical philosophical texts has the potential to enrich social-scientific traditions of self and identity. However, Khatami specifically draws on what he calls 'the last pages of human intellectual history', which he asserts are more relevant in dealing with 'the evolution of philosophical and religious thought'. He explores the theories of Husserl, Descartes, Kant, Marx, Nietzsche, Hume, Freud, Hegel and Fichte, as well as the divine traditions of Christian, Jewish and Muslim thinkers to argue for the need for a dialogue among civilisations, in order to 'free human rights from the bounds of diplomatic negotiations with a discourse for defending human life, dignity and culture'.[3] Khatami's discourse translated into the formation of an international society or in philosophical terms, dialogical communities rather than and apart from existing diplomatic channels.

Dialogue was designed to facilitate communicative action, which would eventually lead to coexistence, tolerance and a degree of cooperation in the global arena. However, Khatami stressed that dialogue could not be based on *Weltanschauung* or belief in philosophical, religious, political or ethical systems. For dialogue to take place efficiently, Khatami maintained, 'we need a set of a priori and comprehensive general axioms, without which dialogue in the precise sense of the word would be impossible'. To this end, he reasoned that 'research in, and articulation of, such axioms and their propagation on a global scale could, and should be undertaken by such venerable institutions as UNESCO'. He argued that the axiomatic foundations of the dialogue among civilisations are in conflict with both the dogmatic axioms of positivists and the absolutes of modernists and post-modernists: 'It is therefore incumbent on thinkers supporting the idea of dialogue among civilisations and cultures to refine its philosophical and theoretical foundations, to safeguard it against the onslaught of dogmatic enmity'.[4]

The discourse was a message to the international community that Iran intended to come out of isolation and to assume a more active role in regional and global affairs. A University of Tehran professor, who closely followed the unfolding of events, emphasised the critical significance of the president's initiative, arguing that it gave Iran 'a specific reputation without which no diplomatic effort on its part would have succeeded in getting substantial results'.[5] It was in this context that Khatami was given recognition in a special resolution by the United Nations General Assembly, declaring 2001 the 'Year of Dialogue Among Civilisations' (see Appendix I). The terms upon which this dialogue won international praise, and contributed to softening the Islamic Republic's image, will be elaborated below. We will also explain why the *Dialogue Among Civilisations* was not a perfectly formed thesis and why it fell short of sufficiently addressing Iran's foreign policy concerns.

Khatami's proposed dialogue was a call for an international public forum that very much mirrored the emerging public space in Iran. In practical terms, Khatami hoped this conceptual paradigm would lead to 'a reduction in international tensions' and 'a détente with the outside world'. It was not only a response to the ineluctable forces of globalisation, but also a new reading of its significance. It was now clear that the intensification of global connectedness in political, economic, social and cultural relations was being driven by the proliferation of media, the means of communication and the increasing ease of travel. These factors equally contributed to economic integration, migration and the information age. As discussed throughout the book, globalisation was largely responsible for demands for greater democratisation and modernisation within Iran.

Greater economic interconnectedness prompted the Iranian establishment – reformists and conservatives alike – to forge a more approachable international image. Pressures emanating from economic globalisation compelled the establishment to assume a more cooperative posture in order to safeguard the country's prosperity. The International Monetary Fund defines the term 'economic globalisation' as follows: 'Economic globalisation is an historical process. This process is the result of human innovation and technological progress and refers to the increasing integration of economies around the world, particularly through trade and financial flows. In this process, individual national economies are being transformed into one global, interdependent economy'.[6] Thus, quite apart from the more humanitarian cause of the 'dialogue among civilisations', Iran's foreign policy direction under Khatami was influenced by the practical need for trade links, foreign capital and expertise, the importance of expatriate resources and the value of diversifying the economy.

New Political Thinking and Foreign Policy

Although Khatami chaired the Supreme National Security Council (the SNSC, the country's top foreign policy body), and selected his chosen foreign and defence ministers (Kharazi and Shamkhani, respectively), he still had to remain wary of domestic sensibilities. While Tehran's new foreign diplomacy was implicitly supported by the *Rahbar*, who declared Iran's relations would be guided by 'dignity, rationality and expediency', this glossed over the fact that the Iranian establishment was acutely divided over key foreign policy issues, especially over relations with the United States, the Arab-Israeli conflict, support for Hizbullah, and nuclear power. At one end of the spectrum of opinion were the ideological conservatives who put Iran's security concerns ahead of all economic or diplomatic considerations. At the other end were the pragmatists who thought it was paramount to rejuvenate Iran from its downward economic spiral if the regime was to survive. On the far end of the spectrum were those who were suspicious of western interference in Iran's affairs, the influence of the Israeli lobby in Washington, and the Zionist movement. In 2001, at the end of Khatami's first term, this defensiveness was articulated by the head of the judiciary, Ayatollah Mahmoud Shahroudi, in these words: 'our national interests lie with antagonising the Great Satan. We condemn any cowardly stance toward America and any word on compromise with the Great Satan'.[7]

It was crucial for Khatami to take the full range of orientations into consideration and to adopt a gradual, incremental approach to easing Iran out of isolation. Khatami focussed on assuring the world that Iran was not bent on regional dominance. Within six months of taking office, he hosted a summit of the Organisation of the Islamic Conference. This was the first effort to end Iran's regional and international isolation and to help improve relations with the Arab world. Using this summit to make new friends, Khatami spelled out his domestic and foreign policy agendas to one of the largest gatherings of Muslim leaders who met to discuss political, economic and social issues. The summit was followed by his famous interview with Christiane Amanpour on CNN (in January 1998), where he called for American-Iranian cultural exchanges among scholars, artists, athletes and tourists. He proclaimed admiration for American political traditions. On the subject of terrorism, Khatami was explicit: 'any form of killing of innocent men and women who are not involved in confrontations is terrorism. It must be condemned, and we, in our turn, condemn every form of it in the world'.[8] Khatami would soon announce that the ten-year *fatwa* (religious decree) ordering the death of Salman Rushdie, author of the controversial book, *The Satanic Verses*, was revoked, signalling a small but significant shift in Iranian policy.

In the wake of Khatami's election and Tehran's new diplomatic tone, European Union governments were eager to resume a 'comprehensive dialogue' with Iran. In February 1998, European Union foreign ministers reached a consensus to lift the ban on top-level contacts with Iran in response to encouraging developments in the country. The foreign ministers stated that they welcomed Khatami's new approach, and that the European Union wished to respond positively to the reformist president's overtures by gradually expanding contact. British Foreign Secretary Robin Cook said it was time to respond to the 'shoots of glasnost' and to take steps to end Iran's political and economic isolation. Soon an agreement by the 15 European Union countries came after pressure from Italy and Greece (which had strong commercial interests in

Iran) for a rapid normalisation of ties, even though Germany and Britain continued to favour a more cautious approach.[9]

Europe was a clear counterweight to Washington and a potential partner in a globalising world. This strategy prompted a flurry of diplomatic activity. Khatami's trip to Paris at the invitation of French President, Jacques Chirac was the first visit to France by an Iranian head of state since the revolution. In 1999, Pope John Paul II gave a private audience to Khatami – the first papal encounter with an Iranian head of state since the days of the Shah.[10] During his stay in Rome, Khatami signed three memoranda of understanding and an economic agreement. Kharazi and his Italian counterpart, Lamberto Dini, signed an agreement for bi-lateral cooperation in an anti-drug campaign, as well as agreements for cooperation in academia and technology.[11] President Jose Maria Aznar visited Iran in 2000, the first visit by a Spanish government leader since the revolution. In 2002, Spanish King Juan Carlos officially welcomed Khatami at his royal palace.[12] In 2004, Prince Charles travelled to Iran to visit the earthquake-destroyed city of Bam; this was the first visit to the country by a member of the British royal family since the revolution.[13] Khatami also met with Home Secretary Jack Straw and visited Vienna on a trip intended to bolster ties with the European Union. Khatami and President Hafez al-Assad of Syria held talks in Damascus, covering Iran's ties with Arab countries and relations with Israel. In a reversal of two decades of animosity, Khatami met in Saudi Arabia with Crown Prince Abdullah, in a move to improve relations – the first visit to Saudi Arabia since the revolution. In 2001, Iran and Saudi Arabia signed an historic security pact for combating crime, terrorism, money laundering and surveillance of borders and territorial waters.[14]

Khatami also made journeys to Central Asia, the Caucasus and the Far East. While Iran, following numerous diplomatic exchanges, struggled to define a coherent policy towards Central Asia and the Caucasus, it became apparent that Khatami was guided by pragmatic concerns and tactical goals rather than blind Islamic revolutionary zeal.[15] He was warmly received in Japan, where he was the first Iranian head of state to visit in 40 years. Khatami met with the Emperor, the prime minister and his cabinet and numerous businessmen and industrialists, and offered a general framework for economic, technological and scientific cooperation between the two countries. On a trip to China, Khatami also stressed the importance of cooperation and asked China to play a more prominent role in Iran and in the Iranian economy. During that visit, the two countries signed memoranda of understanding on economics, energy, industry, culture and science.

Khatami's forays into the international arena resulted in numerous bilateral economic agreements. In 2004, China's state-owned oil trading company, Zhuhai Zhenrong Corporation, signed a 25-year deal to import 110 million tonnes of liquefied natural gas from Iran. This was followed by a $100 million deal between Iran and another of China's state-owned oil companies, signed in 2004.[16] Europe also signed lucrative energy deals with Iran, defying Washington's pressure. In fact, a number of international companies (Total-Fina-Elf, Shell and Repsol) became involved in oil and gas exploration projects in Iranian oilfields. In October 2004, the World Bank approved Iran's request for new infrastructure loans amounting to $220 million, despite Washington's continued opposition.[17] After repeated applications to the World Trade Organisation, Iran succeeded in achieving observer status in 2005, allowing the Iranians to participate in meetings but not in the decision-making process.

During Khatami's second term, Iran's technological and economic relations with Russia expanded considerably. Russian president, Vladimir Putin made nuclear and high-tech cooperation a key component of a broader relationship with Tehran.[18] In 2000, Putin pulled out of the 1995 Gore-Chernomydrin agreement (in which Russia agreed to cease supplying Iran with weapons once existing contracts were filled in 1999) – a significant step towards boosting Russia's relations with Iran.[19] The decision cleared the way for Russian Defence Minister Igor Sergeev to visit Tehran in December 2000 to discuss the resumption of weapons sales. Sergeev and his counterpart discussed arms sales over a ten-year period valued at more than $3 billion. Following Sergeev's visit to Tehran, Khatami accepted Putin's offer and made an official visit to Moscow in March 2001, during which he indicated his desire to purchase more diesel-powered submarines in an effort to boost naval power in the Persian Gulf. In addition, Khatami expressed interest in acquiring TOR-M1 surface-to-air missiles, as well as extended nuclear cooperation. In October 2004, a senior Russian Foreign Ministry official in charge of implementing policy towards Iran expressed that Iran was the only state in the greater Middle East that was rapidly increasing its economic, scientific, technological and military potential.[20]

As a prelude to his candidacy for a second term, Khatami presented the 175-page *Report of the President of the People*, which devoted several pages to his foreign policy achievements. The diplomatic initiatives cited included improving ties with neighbours in the Persian Gulf, Europe, Southeast Asia and Russia, as well with the Central Asian republics (and especially attempts to finalise the legal status of the Caspian Sea); fighting anti-Iranian propaganda; participating in regional and international strategic decisions (for example, OPEC's price stabilisation efforts); participating in 50 international organisations dealing with weapons of mass destruction, environmental protection; signing international treaties against chemical and biological weapons; and winning worldwide praise for the fight against drug trafficking.[21]

In his second presidential term in office, Khatami devoted much energy to allaying the international community's fear about Iran's alleged clandestine nuclear weaponisation programme. On 18 December 2003, Tehran made a pledge of sustained transparency by volunteering to sign the Additional Protocol to the Nuclear Non-proliferation Treaty (NPT). Iran's Ambassador, Ali Salehi signed an Additional Protocol to Iran's NPT safeguards agreement, granting the International Atomic Energy Agency (IAEA) inspectors greater authority in verifying the country's nuclear programme. The Additional Protocol required states to provide an expanded declaration of their nuclear activities and granted the IAEA broader rights of access to sites in the country.[22] Another overture was Iran's temporary suspension of its nuclear fuel cycle – deemed as a 'voluntary' and 'temporary confidence-building' measure under the Paris agreement of November 2004.[23] A report by the American National Intelligence Estimate (NIE) on Iran, released on 3 December 2007, representing the consensus of 16 US intelligence agencies, affirmed that Iran had actually halted its nuclear programme in the autumn of 2003, during Khatami's second term.

Iran-USA: Window of Opportunity?

Khatami and his reformist coalition were unwavering in their support for Iran's right to nuclear technology – a major source of tension between Iran and the United States. There were also many other serious issues dividing the two countries. Khatami's administration supported the Palestinian cause and opposed the Jewish lobby over American policy towards Iran. Moreover, they cited an end to sanctions and the unfreezing of Iranian assets as preconditions to holding official deliberations. In his 27 May 1997 press conference – his first with foreign reporters and carried live by CNN – Khatami vehemently rejected accusations that Iran was involved in terrorism and weapons of mass destruction. In relation to the Arab-Israeli conflict, Khatami asserted, 'Of course, we are not going to have any intervention in this matter and we are going to leave it to the people of Palestine and the governments and the people of the region'. He added, 'but we do keep the right to express our views regarding the matter … and with a scientific, realistic approach we do think that the current process will not come to any conclusion'. Khatami firmly stated that Iran would neither recognise Israel nor negotiate with it. In his words, 'we believe that there can be no peace until all the legitimate demands of the Palestinians are met'. Khatami blamed Iranian-American hostility on Washington: 'As long as the US is after harming Iran's interests and independence, Iran will have no relations with the US'.[24]

Khatami's tone was distinctly more conciliatory when he extended an olive branch to the American people in his CNN interview with Christiane Amanpour. Following the interview, Washington slightly softened its tone towards Tehran. In May 1998, Washington announced that it would waive the provisions of the 1996 Iran-Libya Sanctions Act (ILSA) against a consortium of French, Russian and Malaysian companies, in return for Europe agreeing to press Iran about terrorism and weapons of mass destruction.[25] On 17 June 1998, Secretary of State Madeleine Albright delivered a major speech that addressed almost point-by-point the issues Khatami had raised in his CNN interview with Amanpour. The speech was notable for avoiding the heated rhetoric, which had characterised American statements about Iran. Albright's speech did not offer any specific new policies, but it projected the prospect of a new beginning:

> We are ready to explore further ways to build mutual confidence and avoid misunderstandings. The Islamic Republic should consider parallel steps … As the wall of mistrust comes down, we can develop with the Islamic Republic, when it is ready, a road map leading to normal relations. Obviously two decades of mistrust cannot be erased overnight. The gap between us remains wide. But it is time to test the possibilities for bridging this gap.[26]

The United States removed Iran from the list of states subject to sanctions for dealing in narcotics. It no longer identified Iran as the leading sponsor of terrorism (although Iran remained on the list of states sponsoring terrorism). Moreover, it formally designated the Iranian exile opposition group *Mojahedin-e Khalq* as a terrorist organisation. A number of small changes were adopted to make American visas easier to obtain for Iranians, and in 1999, sanctions inhibiting the sale of food and medicine to Iran were removed. Perhaps even more significant, President Clinton made a series of statements in which he recognised positive changes in Iran's policies. He acknowledged that Iran had legitimate grievances because of the past involvement of external powers in its domestic affairs. These overtures represented an important shift in American foreign policy during Khatami's first two years in office.

Following the 2000 parliamentary elections in Iran, Secretary Albright acknowledged American involvement in the coup that overthrew the democratically elected Iranian Prime Minister, Mohammad Mossadeq, in 1953. She also discussed American grievances towards Iran, but welcomed the prospect of 'regional discussions aimed at reducing tensions and building trust'.[27] She added that the time had come 'for America and Iran to enter a new season in which mutual trust may grow and a quality of warmth supplant the long, cold winter of our mutual discontent'. This was the most far-reaching expression of American interest in rapprochement since the revolution. Behzad Nabavi, a key supporter of President Khatami in the Sixth *Majles*, praised Albright's speech and concluded that it was a kind of victory and an achievement for Khatami's government.[28]

Nevertheless, mutual hostility was soon to be suddenly elevated to a new high under President George W. Bush, when in his State of the Union address in January 2002 he grouped Iran, Iraq and North Korea together as an 'axis of evil'. He alleged that Iran was a sponsor of terrorism, and a threat to Israel and its neighbours for its pursuit of weapons of mass destruction. Bush's proposals on how to deal with Iran spanned from the possibility of a pre-emptive military strike, covert action to destabilise the ruling regime, assistance to internal and external opposition groups, financial aid for foreign-based Iranian media, and a call for international condemnation of the Iranian leadership.[29] The irony in this collective label and policy was that Washington failed to differentiate between Khatami and Saddam Hussein. Saddam Hussein was a tyrant who openly challenged the United States, while Khatami disagreed with Washington's hawkish policies in the Middle East. In fact, Khatami had opposed the rule of the Taliban in Afghanistan and he had actively supported the Northern Alliance. In the autumn of 2001, Iran supported US military action against the Taliban in Afghanistan. Iran also participated in the post-war Bonn Conference of December 2001, where the transitional governing authority for Afghanistan was established. Former US special envoy to Afghanistan, James Dobbins, commented that Iran had in fact played a constructive role in the Bonn conference by advising that the Bonn agreement contain phrasing calling for democracy. After the collapse of the Taliban, Khatami supported the new government under Hamed Karzai, and encouraged cooperation between Iran and Afghanistan.[30]

The classification of Iran as part of the 'axis of evil' offended Iranian radicals and reformers alike.[31] The reformers were pushing to open up the country's political milieu for negotiation with Washington over their differences. Ignorant of the political conditions and the nature of reform movement in Iran, Washington disappointed the reformers. Its closing of the door to

Iran paved the way for the proliferation of increasingly anti-American sentiments. In fact, it would be fair to argue that Bush's crude threats since 2002 served to change the domestic debate in Iran, radicalising borderline 'conservative-moderates' who had not completely dismissed the possibility of a dialogue with the US government. Khatami was not bent on creating a pan-Islamic revolution, and he had proved this to the international community. The United States failed to grasp that Khatami was a pragmatic and rational man, and that they could have engaged in meaningful dialogue. In fact, Khatami represented an opportunity that the American government might have converted to their own interests, but instead turned their back on.

The Limits of Dialogue

Ray Takeyh makes the argument that Washington failed to capitalise on the opportunity to negotiate with a moderate president in power in Iran.[32] This is a fair point; however, it is presumptuous to assume that the United States and Iran would have mended fences by opening up a dialogue. On a broad range of strategic and ideological issues, Washington and Tehran were, and remain, fundamentally at odds. For example, although Khatami and his reformist ministers announced a policy of non-intervention in relation to the Arab-Israeli peace process, they opposed the American-brokered peace effort and offered material support to the Palestinians in their struggle against Israel. On various occasions, Khatami reiterated Iran's support for Hizbullah's guerrilla group, which he once described as 'an ideological and humanitarian movement'.[33] The reformists also firmly supported Iran's legitimate right to nuclear power.[34]

The *Dialogue Among Civilisations* was a noble cause. It was a simple message, but it resonated throughout the world. It was important to see an Iranian leader carry the flag of dialogue and solidarity among nations. Sending out a message of hope and understanding, the *Dialogue* sent out a positive image of Iran to the world. However, it is essential to understand that Iran's problems with the outside world – its nuclear dossier, its resistance to US hegemony in the Middle East, its support for Hamas and Hizbullah, its relations with regional Arab rivals – had nothing to do with cultural or civilisational differences. These foreign policy issues were based purely on strategic considerations and national interest – explicitly, Iran's primary concern was, and remains, its security, its territorial integrity, its political independence and its independent cultural identity. Iran's conduct in the international arena has been a product of these considerations. Even if the channels of communication between Iran and the USA were opened, it would have taken much more than a dialogue to resolve historical grievances between the two countries, and to reach consensus on diverging positions. In this context, it is clear that a dialogue would not have resolved serious, day-to-day foreign policy issues involving Iran, the USA, the international community and the Arab states.

Indeed, from the outset, there were serious limits to achieving constructive dialogue with the west through the philosophical project of the *Dialogue Among Civilisations*. To begin with, the objectives of the enterprise were not clearly defined. Was the goal to be the attainment of some tangible political benefits, albeit through a philosophical project? For instance, was the enterprise intended to normalise relations, particularly between the USA and Iran? If so, the project was doomed to fail from the start because Khatami did not represent the will of the entire political establishment. Most conservatives would have never entertained the idea of establishing dialogue, let alone diplomatic political relations with the Islamic Republic's arch-enemy. As stressed earlier, for such a vision to have any chance of materialising, Khatami would have had to foster internal dialogue and consultation between opposing camps.

In the same vein, it can be argued that the project of dialogue, though frequently talked about and referred to, failed to enter the arena of ideas and philosophy. Many a time, Khatami supported the *Dialogue* thesis by drawing from Islamic and western values emphasising intellectual engagement. However, the dialogue, which was supposed to include academics, NGOs, governments and artists, never actually entered the realm of ideas. Substance needed to be added to the rhetoric and this could only be achieved through analysis, discussion and critique of the thesis and the project, usually beyond the patience of politicians. Here, a serious methodological shortcoming can be pinpointed, as such an ambitious task could never be carried forwards only through rhetoric.

Another issue had to do with the ambiguity and the imprecise nature of civilisational themes, which often led to vague conclusions. In many of his documented speeches, Khatami stated that the *Dialogue* was about talking and listening, and that the east and the west were partners in this dialogue. Dialogue, he said, is carried out to discover the truth and to find salvation, understanding and coexistence. This is an axiological view of dialogue: it is aimed at discovering truth and in finding salvation. That renders the task of those not sharing the views very difficult, particularly as there is no such thing as a universally agreed upon definition or interpretation of truth. The same question applies to the notion of salvation.

Philosophical questions aside, the *Dialogue* was ultimately a political thesis and as such intended to affect political change on an international scale. One serious criticism that can be levelled against the thesis is its practicality and functionality. Was the *Dialogue* a conceptual paradigm that could ultimately be translated into policies at the state level? The nature of world politics is state-centric; policies are formulated by states and not by civilisations. States act primarily according to national interests, and at times strategic and national interests have priority over civilisational, cultural or religious bonds. Even the Islamic Republic has at times placed survival of the regime and the nation ahead of its ideational convictions. For instance, in the dispute between Azerbaijan and Armenia over Nogorno-Karabakh, Iran tilted more in favour of Christian Armenia than Muslim Azerbaijan. Thus, bearing in mind the predominance of state-centrism, it would appear baseless to propound civilisational themes.

Was the *Dialogue Among Civilisations* a general rapprochement between political Islam and the west? If this was the case, Iran does not represent the Islamic world. The only country in the world with *Shi'i* Islam as its state religion, Iran is viewed by the many *Sunni* countries with suspicion, and they clash on many geo-political, strategic and religious issues. This factor is further complicated by the historical animosity between Persians and Arabs. As such, Khatami was unable to represent the entire Muslim world because he lacked sufficient support from the *Sunni* Arab states for his project. Therefore, if Khatami was intending to represent the global Islamic platform in the dialogue with the west, he lacked the coherence and unity to do so.

It should also be noted that another important factor that worked in direct conflict with the project of the *Dialogue Among Civilisations* was the course of international political developments. The events of 11 September 2001 appeared to strengthen Huntington's clash of civilisations thesis rather than Khatami's counter-thesis. The perpetrators of the tragic events were not representative of any state but members of non-state terrorist organisations. In this context, the state system and the structure of the state-centric world became less relevant and it seemed that only a Huntingtonian framework could explain the horrific events. A once receptive international audience began to show much less interest in hearing messages of dialogue and peace from a Muslim leader, or in showing faith in the idea of inter-civilisational harmony. Amid this confusion, a blow was struck against the *Dialogue*, ironically in the same year that the UN had declared the 'Year of Dialogue Among Civilisations'.

During his tenure, Khatami ushered in a new foreign policy direction that focused on diplomatic dialogue, expanding trade and cooperative security measures. The discourse of the *Dialogue Among Civilisations* set the stage for a new international public forum. Khatami repeatedly demonstrated that ideological dogma was inconsistent with the reformist perspective and of limited use in a globalising age. Acting as a rational international actor with a matching rhetoric, Khatami established cordial relations with key international players in the European Union, Saudi Arabia and the Far East, bringing important diplomatic exchanges to the country. While the barometer of change in Iran for the United States seems to be limited to Iran's support for Hizbullah, it can be safely concluded that in foreign relations Khatami's accomplishments were notable. However, it is crucial to recognise that the proposed dialogue could achieve only so much: during Khatami's eight-year presidency, Iran's key foreign policy concerns and points of contention with the outside world remained unsettled, albeit in large part due to the intractability of the issues. However, this is not to suggest that the *Dialogue Among Civilisations* was a perfectly formed thesis. There were also serious methodological shortcomings to the *Dialogue* itself, in terms of both substance and practical application.

This section has briefly touched on the validity of the paradigm and its ability to effect change; what became evident is that the project lacked the practical underpinnings required to bring about substantive change in the global arena. The discourse of the *Dialogue Among Civilisations* must be recognised for what it is: a utopian, romanticised worldwide cause; and in this capacity did it prove to be a commendable thesis.

The showcase of Khatami's presidency, the *Dialogue Among Civilisations* was designed to arrive at specific targeted objectives. While it was based on a principled position, it was squarely founded on political calculation and instinct. A perfect sound bite, the *Dialogue* was also a clever political tactic based on hard calculation. It represented a trend of thought and a strategy designed to make political capital out of a complicated political situation. In the first place, the discourse was extended to the west in order to obtain maximum economic concessions from western countries as the only solution to the acute economic crisis. Another calculation was based on political survival instinct: Khatami sought to use foreign policy gains to move up the ladder in the balance of power within the regime. Cognizant of his own and his cabinet's inability to resolve an array of economic and social problems confronting the regime – especially during his second term – foreign policy achievements were the only bargaining chips Khatami had in his dealings with the rival faction.

While it was undeniable that Khatami and his faction used a different tone and a different approach in the international arena, there was no road map to resolving conflicts, nor was there an agenda for negotiating or settling macro-political issues. In order to bring Iran out of isolation and to attempt to normalise relations, Khatami needed a framework that consisted of multiple steps, processes, levels of involvement, stakeholders and issues. The *Dialogue* did not go far beyond an exercise in rhetoric and conventional diplomacy. As we have mentioned, Iranian foreign policy was based on certain immutable convictions and positions.

Iran would not compromise on these issues, which it deems vital to its national interest. The international community rejected many of these positions, and Khatami was well are aware of these points of contention. To extend foreign relations, Iran had to go beyond dialogue, or rather compliment dialogue with vigorous lobbying for engagement. For this, Khatami needed a road map to go hand in hand with the attractive new discourse he was presenting to the world.

In a round table discussion at the United Nations in 2000 (see Appendix II), Khatami elaborated on the *Dialogue Among Civilisations* by outlining the features of a global utopia where cultures and identities interact and co-exist in harmony and unity. He explained that the glue binding the world's diverse cultures and civilisations consists of 'empathy, compassion and understanding'. In accordance with the principles of participatory society, he urged citizens' participation, without which there would be the danger of 'cultural homelessness' where people would be deprived of solace both in their own culture and in the 'vast open horizon on global culture'. The presentation is telling as it embodies the words of a cleric, at times sounding more like a sermon than a political speech. In practical terms, Khatami's prescription for global change was unrealistic, espousing a romantic, idealistic view of the world. The presentation, however, is an excellent narrative in its capacity to motivate humankind to find inspiration in building a better future. Khatami knew how to appeal to a broad audience, by using stirring catchwords and by imbuing his rhetoric with hope and faith. At his core, Khatami was more of an inspirational holy man than a politician. His speeches and discussions expose his essence and his mindset, and explain why Khatami was so far from finding a practical solution – that essential road map – to integrating Iran with the world.

6

OBSTACLES TO REFORM

The historian of the Middle East, Ira Lapidus, has written:

> Iran is a nation that is open and welcoming but remains hidden and mysterious; a clerical dictatorship but one of the Middle East's liveliest democracies, a puritanical regime but a people who love everyday life; a severe orthodoxy but an expressive cinema and an argumentative press; a revolution that has rejected secularism but a nation heading toward a fusion of Islamic and Persian identities.[1]

Khatami's political movement, in its attempt to combine Islamic traditionalism (chiefly characterised by opposition to secularism and certain western social norms) with European liberalism (pluralism, the rule of law, civil society and citizenship), may be added to Lapidus's list of paradoxes. The movement was 'modern' and rational in the sense that it proposed reform of Islamic thought through emphasis on independent reason, rather than *taqlid* (blind emulation of the conservative *ulama* deemed the paragon of moral excellence). At the same time, the movement was 'traditional' in its commitment to a theocracy with Islamic institutions governed by figures with superior Islamic credentials. The ambivalent nature of this blueprint was mirrored in the Iranian political system. This chapter will show that given the nature of Iran's distinctive political institutions, Khatami's strong mandate did not translate into strong executive powers. In fact, as already shown, two contradictory forces were at work in Iran: one led by the president, who aspired to distribute power across a democratised Iranian society, and the other led by the conservative elite who sought to centralise power in the Iranian political apparatus.

This chapter makes the case that the reform movement failed in part to reach maturity due to the conservative reaction and Khatami's failure to bridge the political divide. In order to explain how this force obstructed Khatami's efforts to implement reform (particularly in relation to domestic issues) it is first necessary to describe the political organisation of the Islamic Republic. It will be argued here that the power struggle between the reformist camp and the conservative block reflects the discrepancy between Iran's democratically elected offices and its unelected institutions. This will become particularly evident in describing the tactics used by the conservative faction to curtail the Second of Khordad Movement (23 May 1997, the day commemorating Khatami's first presidential victory). This chapter will demonstrate how the reaction affected Khatami's approach to reforms, rendering him both passive and active, reformist and conformist.

Paradoxes of the Power Structure

The Islamic Republic's power structure is characterised by a multitude of loosely connected and fiercely opposed competitive power centres, both formal and informal. The former are grounded in the constitution and in government regulations, and take the form of the state institutions and offices. The latter is comprised of informal religio-political organisations, foundations and paramilitary groups, mainly aligned with the conservative camp. The duality of power runs like a thread through nearly all of the political spheres of the Islamic Republic, and is partly responsible for the incoherence in the country's policies. Moreover, because of the unequal distribution of power among the branches of government, the Iranian polity is riddled with inefficiencies, factionalism and systemic paradoxes.

The formal political structure can be divided into elected and unelected bodies. The president, his cabinet and the parliament are elected directly, while the core of the regime, including the Supreme Leader, the Expediency Discernment Council, the Council of Ministers, the Guardian Council, the Assembly of Experts, the judiciary and the commanders of the IRGC, are unelected bodies.

The second most powerful official in Iran is the president, who is responsible for the daily affairs of the country. The president's responsibilities focus primarily on social and economic issues, not on foreign policy, even though he chairs the Supreme National Security Council, an influential 12-member committee that coordinates government activities related to defence, the intelligence services and foreign policy. The president, who is popularly elected for a four-year term, also selects a cabinet (with the approval of the legislature), appoints members of the Expediency Discernment Council, and controls the Planning and Budget Organisation, which gives him great sway over economic policy. In addition, the president appoints the governor of the Central Bank. The president and his ministers can be removed only through a two-thirds majority no-confidence vote in the *Majles.*

It is important to understand that the president does not determine the overarching guidelines of Iranian foreign policy. This authority is vested by the constitution in the *velayat-e faqih* – the strongest power centre in Iran. Under Article 110 of the constitution, the Supreme Leader has primary control over state organs and enjoys the right to appoint key officials, such as six members of the powerful Guardian Council and the heads of the judiciary, the broadcast media, the armed forces and various revolutionary bodies. He also confirms the president's election.

The incumbent Supreme Leader, Ayatollah Khamenei, had control of the security apparatus, consisting of the IRGC and the regular forces (the two bodies are under a joint general command). The IRGC had a powerful presence in other institutions, controlling volunteer militias with branches in every town. Khamenei was responsible for appointing the heads and staff of various informal power circles – religious supervisory bodies that serve as the extended arms of the *vali-e faqih.* These groups are entrusted to ensure that the religiousness of the regime remains intact. This group includes representatives of the Supreme Leader, the Association of Friday Prayer Leaders, *sazmanha-ye aqidati-siyasi* (ideological–political organisations), *Dadgah-he Vizheh-ye Rouhaniyat* (the Special Court for the Clergy, which deals with offences committed by the clergy), *anjomanha-ye Islami* (the Islamic associations), revolutionary organisations, the *bonyad* (including the

Foundation of the Disinherited, the Fifteenth of Khordad Foundation and the Martyr Foundation), the *Basij* militia (who are under the IRGC), religious security forces, revolutionary committees and the media. These organisations have the extra-legal right to intervene, directly or indirectly, in the affairs of the country, and the central government exercises little or no control over them. Owing to their strong religious inclinations, these bodies are almost above government.

The Supreme Leader is chosen by the clerics who make up the Assembly of Experts. This body not only appoints the Supreme Leader, it also monitors his performance and can in theory unseat him if he is deemed incapable of fulfilling his duties. The assembly holds two sessions a year, and although the body's headquarters are based in Qom, sessions are held in Tehran and Mashhad. Although the 86 members of the assembly are voted in for a term of eight years, only clerics can join the assembly, and the Guardian Council vets candidates for election. Conservatives dominated the assembly during Khatami's presidency.

Although the *vali-e faqih* rarely intervenes in the affairs of the executive, he monitors its policies through a network of clerical commissars of the Supreme Leader. Without cooperation between the Supreme Leader and president, progress and stability are seriously hampered. The tension between the office of the Supreme Leader who controls foreign policy, and the president who chairs the Supreme National Security Council, is clear. This is why it has been argued here that the process of political reform precipitated and instigated by Khatami had to have been implicitly endorsed by the Supreme Leader – at least in the first few years of his tenure. However, it is also true that in Khatami's Iran, the country's highest office was filled by a Supreme Leader who played a deciding role in the factional struggle that ensued shortly after the 1997 reformist electoral landslide by publicly supporting the conservative faction. In turn, the conservative right strongly upheld the supremacy of the religious dimension of the regime over its republicanism, and espoused an absolutist reading of the *velayat-e faqih*.[2]

One of the most influential bodies in Iran is the unelected Guardian Council, composed of six theologians appointed by the Supreme Leader, and six lay jurists nominated by the judiciary and approved by parliament. The Council is effectively an upper house of parliament. The highest vetting organ of the country, the Guardian Council is designated to review all laws passed by the *Majles*, and to veto any laws that it judges do not comply with Islamic laws or Iran's constitution. Members are elected for six years on a phased basis, so that half the membership changes every three years. The Council can bar candidates from running in elections to parliament, the presidency and the Assembly of Experts. It is able to reject without the right of appeal those that it judges to be unqualified or of unsuitable character. Since the 1979 revolution, the conservative right has occupied seats in the Guardian Council and used the powers of this super-body to bar reformist candidates from running for the Seventh *Majles* in 2004. The religious 'superbody', the Expediency Discernment Council (comprised of jurists from the Guardian Council and selected government officials), resolves disputes between the Council and the *Majles*. The Expediency Council is an arbitration body that settles disputes between the legislature and the Guardian Council over laws, and makes the final decision binding. The Supreme Leader appoints its members, who are prominent religious, social and political figures. On 18 March 1997, Khamenei appointed 27 new members for five years and Rafsanjani as Chairman.

The directly elected *Majles*, the institution that would typically enact laws in a republic, shares its decisions with the Guardian Council. The constitution actually stipulates that without the existence of the Guardian Council, the *Majles* is devoid of sovereignty. The unicameral *Majles* is made up of 290 members who are elected by the direct vote of the people for four years. Elections are held on a multi-member constituency basis, with voters casting as many votes as there are seats in parliament allotted to their constituency. All candidates must be approved by the Guardian Council. After a bill or a motion is tabled, debating procedure begins with the first reading of a bill. Should the bill's generalities be passed in the first reading, it would then be forwarded to the committee(s) concerned for a review of its details and amendments. The bill then comes up for a second reading, where details and amendments are either accepted or rejected. At this stage, members of the *Majles* whose proposed amendments have not been adopted by the committee concerned may put their proposal to the full House and call for votes. If the bill is passed in the second reading, it is goes back to the Guardian Council, which ultimately decides if the bill is suitable for ratification.

The conservatives' main agent was the judiciary, a body that essentially ensures theocratic predominance. Consisting of a Supreme Court, a Supreme Judicial Council and lower courts, the judiciary ensures that *sharia* laws are enforced. The chief justice and the prosecutor general must be *mujtahids* (*Shi'i* jurists). The judiciary nominates the six lay members of the Guardian Council. The head of the judiciary is appointed by, and reports to the Supreme Leader. The conservatives routinely used the judicial system to undermine reforms. Until Ayatollah Khomeini's death in 1989, the judiciary was largely controlled by radicals and left-wingers. Since then, this body has been connected with the conservative camp under its former head, Mohammad Yazdi. In order to speed up procedures, Yazdi created general courts in which the presiding judge is also the prosecutor, and has total power. In 1999, the head of the judiciary was replaced by Ayatollah Shahroudi. In 2000, when accused by the parliamentary majority of having violated the constitution and the laws in force, he justified himself by arguing that only members of the clergy were entitled to interpret legal texts.[3]

Iran's power centres are made up of a combination of the Islamic-revolutionary elite composed of *Shi'i* clerics and laypersons. The battle lines, however, are not completely clear. Iran's political scene is vastly more complex than the simple divisions between 'reformists' and 'conservatives', or 'moderates' and 'hard-liners' that are used in the media. Although the elite can be loosely grouped into two ideological factions, each category encompasses a broad set of groups, each with its own ideology and world-view. When the actual power distribution in Iran and the ideological makeup of the religious super-bodies are taken into account, it is evident that the reformists, despite enjoying a massive popular mandate, had in fact extremely limited structural power. The conservative faction had the institutional upper hand and used this power to weaken and discredit the reform movement, which they perceived as threatening Iran's social harmony and the essence of the Islamic Republic. Some causes were less noble. Some deeply entrenched conservatives were motivated by power aspirations and financial interests. Khatami, on the other hand, enjoyed the support of a broad coalition of politically aware groups, buttressed by a burgeoning youth culture, an educated middle class and socially conscious women – all craving social freedoms and economic security. This was a potent and synergetic force that made political change in Iran inevitable. The conservatives recognised this, and in turn waged a repressive campaign against the new president's reform agenda. As a result, many Iranians who were once optimistic about the Reform Movement became sorely disappointed, while some other supporters directed their frustration at Khatami for not overcoming the conservative challenges to his proposals.[4]

Political Resistance

Immediately after the 1997 election, the conservative camp went on the offensive. The response to the new ideological challenge posed by the Second of Khordad Movement was to take refuge in the country's religiousness. For Ayatollah Abdolqasem Khazali nothing was more deplorable than religious pluralism and the suggestion that the essence of religion could be debated outside the seminary.[5] An editorial in a leading conservative daily reminded the public that human-made laws were inherently flawed, and hence the need for the supervision of the *faqih*. Other dailies reiterated that unlike other political offices, the Supreme Leader was a holy appointee and not directly elected.[6] Among other prominent clerics, Ayatollah Abdollah Javad Amoli fiercely contested the notion of a democratically elected *faqih*. He was clear in taking the unassailability of the *faqih* to new heights: 'This [democratic practice] implies that the society is entitled to unseat and appoint even the prophets. How, then, do we respond to the Qur'anic verses?'[7]

The more radical elements of the establishment were profoundly suspicious of the western variety of democracy, believing that it would undermine the moral foundation of the Iranian-Islamic revolution.[8] They constantly lamented that under Khatami, the revolution's values were fading and that Islam was being desecrated. The Allied Islamic Society went so far as to suggest that some groups, infatuated with western ideas, were implicitly seeking to rid the country of its Islamic roots.[9] *Ansar-e Hizbullah* accused Khatami of being a westernised liberal, and conceded that their support for Khatami was strictly due to respect for the Supreme Leader.[10] Khamenei himself issued a stern warning to the Second of Khordad Front, reaffirming that his rule was derived from the Qur'an, the sayings of the Prophet and the Imams, thus distancing his sacred authority from theirs and implying that unquestioned obedience to the *faqih* was a religious duty. The Supreme Leader also scorned secularising forces for plotting against Islam and the regime: 'The epoch of adhering to western prescriptions has passed. The enemies of Islam are seeking to separate religion from politics. Using seductive western concepts such as political participation, competitive pluralist political systems, and bogus democracy, the westernised are trying to present a utopic picture of western societies and portray them as the only salvation for our Islamic society'.[11]

Khatami's unprecedented popular mandate was no match for the institutional might of the conservatives who had a firm grip on the country's power bases. His election laid bare the reality that the hierarchical structure of the Iranian state was a powerful counterweight to popular will. The election demonstrated that Iran's dual-natured political system made the country prone to factionalism, which in turn, led to inertia and stagnation. Khatami's lack of real power was referred to regularly by the pro-reformist press, often in disputing the legitimacy of the conservatives' power, and lowering the public's expectations in the process. Mehdi Karroubi, who was the secretary of the Society of Combatant Clerics, was typical. He publicised the reality Khatami faced, particularly the panoply of difficulties he had in implementing his reforms due to lack of cooperation from various state organisations.[12]

The conservatives, nevertheless, were unable to damage Khatami's popular image or to discredit his democratic message. They made extensive use of their institutional-legal privileged position to purge the president's closest allies. The attack's first victim was Mayor Karbaschi, who had campaigned actively for Khatami in 1997. As mentioned earlier, Karbaschi had placed the entire machinery of the municipal government at the service of Khatami's campaigners during the election. Karbaschi was immensely popular in Tehran and as mayor was recognised for his efficiency and achievements. He was now charged with embezzlement and squandering public money and, along with a number of his deputies, he was arrested in April 1998. Three months later, the court sentenced Karbaschi to five years imprisonment, and barred him from public office for ten years.[13] His sentence was soon reduced to two years after an appeal. The successful destruction of Tehran's widely popular mayor signalled the beginning of the judiciary's efforts (headed by the ultra-conservative Mohammad Yazdi until 1999) in subjugating the Second of Khordad Movement. It was the opening powerful shot marking its intention to fully enter into the factional battleground.

The Karbaschi debacle was soon followed by an even more aggressive move. Abdollah Nouri was a steadfast reformer in charge of the government's most important executive body, the Ministry of Interior, and was perceived as a threat by many conservatives. He had immediately removed many rightist officials in the ministry and quickly became the object of the right's wrath. He had also refused to dismiss Karbaschi – a stance seen to conflict overtly with the wishes of the Supreme Leader. While all these factors contributed to Nouri's removal, it was the offence of his support for Ayatollah Montazeri that the Supreme Leader could not overlook.[14] Led by Mohammad Reza Bahonar, 31 parliamentary ministers appealed for Nouri's impeachment. They accused him of being unable to maintain social peace, causing unrest in the country by his support for Karbaschi, and making unsuitable appointments in the Ministry of Interior. A slim majority of 137 ministers voted for his removal, while 117 voted against the motion, with 11 abstentions. Mehdi Moslem contends that the conservative campaign actually backfired, making Karbaschi and Nouri 'martyrs' of democracy and Khatami the 'oppressed'.[15]

As the scope of the psychological war widened, the pro-Khatami press began reporting a much more organised and sweeping scheme to eliminate the civil society project. The speculation and indeed fear among Khatami's people was that the extremists' ultimate goal was to oust Khatami through a political coup. After all, the conservatives had powerful and varied means to discredit and intimidate Khatami's allies and pro-reform activists. The conservative daily *Kayhan*, and its editor Hossein Shariatmadari, championed the ideological crusade of the far right through the press. The religious justification for the campaign against the reformists was furnished by ultra-conservative clerics like Yazdi who attacked the press for diluting the concept of the *velayat-e faqih*. Similarly, the deputy of the IRGC, Mohammad Baqer Zolqadr, enlisted the support of the IRGC with this statement: 'IRGC will react swiftly to anything that would threaten this holy regime', and added that the IRGC reserved the right to engage in the non-military affairs of the country.[16] Khamenei offered the support of the highest institution – the *velayat-e faqih* – aligning himself with the conservative bloc.

The power struggle took on a particularly sinister tone in autumn 1998 when four dissident intellectuals were brutally murdered. The manner of their deaths had been particularly gruesome, sending shockwaves throughout Iranian society. Khatami promptly launched an investigation and squarely pointed the finger at the Ministry of Intelligence, who acknowledged that its agents were involved in the murders. Subsequently, 18 people were arrested and tried in connection with the murders. On 20 June 1999, the prosecutor of the Judicial Complex for the Armed Forces announced the mastermind was Saeed Emami, a high-ranking official of the Ministry of Information, who committed suicide while in custody.[17]

Gholamhussein Mohseni Ezhei, Minister of Intelligence and the presiding judge in the Karbaschi affair, supervised the prosecutions of leading reformist clerics and Khatami's closest allies: Abdollah Nouri and Mohsen Kadivar. In March 1999, the court accused cleric, philosopher and activist Kadivar with disturbing public opinion, based on a speech in which he discussed the motives of those responsible for the serial murders. The court charged him with 'propaganda against the sacred system of the Islamic Republic' following an interview in which Kadivar made the controversial statement that the structures of the Shah's government remained intact. The court sentenced him to 18 months in prison on both charges.[18] In November 1999, the Special Court for the Clergy convicted the impeached Minister of Interior, Nouri, who was also publisher of the *Khordad* newspaper, on charges that his newspaper published articles, which 'defamed the system' and spread propaganda against the state. He was sentenced to five years in prison.[19]

Earlier in 1999, Nouri and the Minister of Islamic Culture and Guidance, Mohajerani, were beaten up by a group that allegedly belonged to radical elements of Hizbullah.[20] The violent face of the conservative reaction included the attempted assassination of Saeed Hajjarian, one of Khatami's closest allies, considered by many to be the mastermind strategist of the reform movement; the imprisonment of prominent reformists, including Mohsen Sazegara, Abbas Abdi, and investigative journalists Akbar Ganji and Emadedin Baghi; and the trial and death sentence of Hashem Aghajari, a university professor and political activist accused of insulting Islamic values during one of his speeches. The death sentence was reversed after widespread protests by students and reformist parties. Aghajari was released after a brief stay in prison.[21]

The 9 July 1999 student uprising (which came to be known as the Eighteenth of Tir Student Uprising) marked a turning point in the evolution of the reaction. On the evening of 8 July 1999, some 200 students staged a peaceful protest in front of their dormitories at the Koo-ye Daaneshgaah-e Tehran. In general, student demands and slogans called on the government to live up to its promise of a civil society and to promote good government, democracy and pluralism. The Supreme Leader and many officials affiliated with the conservative faction, conservative newspapers such as *Resaalat* and *Kayhan*, and the *Ansar-e Hizbullah*, were frequent targets of attack by students and were often mentioned by name. Students regularly demanded the release of political prisoners. There were references to economic inequalities, social justice and political democracy, but none bore the mark of any specific ideological camp such as socialism, capitalism or Marxism. There were a number of slogans demanding Islamic justice and using Islamic symbolism to call for transparency, accountability, integrity and justice in the government.

The protest groups were forcibly dispersed and returned to campus. According to reports, early in the morning, 'an organised force of some 400 men – wearing uniforms of black trousers and white shirts and carrying distinctive blue batons – broke into the dormitories, systematically ransacked student rooms, and assaulted students indiscriminately'.[22] The attacks were massive and the damage was vast. The students themselves were not the only targets of the brutality. Rooms were searched, personal property destroyed, cash found in the rooms was stolen, and pictures and books were torn or burned. Ten buildings and 800 rooms were damaged. Windows in nearby houses and cars were broken. Iranian newspapers reported that five people were killed and dozens more wounded.[23] Security forces denied the killing, but acknowledged one death and three injured. The damage, however, was so extensive that it could neither be covered up nor left without a response. Government officials and religious leaders began to offer their apologies to the students for what had taken place. The Minister of Culture and Higher Education, the Chancellor of the University of Tehran, as well as the heads of 18 colleges offered their resignations in protest. Khatami condemned the raid and asked for calm. The news of the attack brought thousands of students together in protest, first in the University of Tehran, and later in universities in eight other cities. The Islamic Student Association of the University of Tehran condemned the attack and called for a sit-in protest on campus.[24]

In July 2001, the court convicted the students and sentenced them to prison terms of six months to a year, labelling them 'hooligans'.[25] A majority of 159 *Majles* deputies submitted a petition to the judiciary, criticising 'the transformation of victims into the guilty party'.[26] Student organisations severely criticised the judiciary and complained that the laws of the state were being perverted to work against the reformist political movement. They complained the verdicts were 'worse than the blows in the dormitories … even than being killed'.[27] The showdown resulted in widespread criticism of Khatami, who was accused of being too passive. The fact was that Khatami may have been relatively quiet during the debacle but it was a major political risk for him to be too vocal as the opposition would be quick to label him as a secularist liberal and question his allegiance to the Islamic Republic. Overall, the incident was seen as something of a fiasco and reflected badly upon

Khatami; the Minister of Interior himself admitted that he did not have full control over the police, despite his designated position as commander-in-chief of the force on behalf of the Supreme Leader.[28]

Another blow to the reform movement occurred on 23 April 2000 when, within a span of two weeks, the conservative judiciary shut down 18 out of 20 pro-reform publications on charges of anti-revolutionary writings.[29] An anonymous judiciary official explained that a committee formed to investigate the press had concluded that 'despite frequent warnings given to them [the press], they continued with their anti-Islamic and anti-revolutionary activities'. He added that the 'tone of the material in those papers had brought smiles to the faces of the enemies of the Islamic Republic and hurt the feelings of devout Muslims at home and even the leader of the Islamic revolution'.[30] In fact, there was no consensus in the *Majles* on what was considered constructive criticism, and what was perceived as a threat to national interest. Khamenei immediately put a stop to the parliamentarians' debate on the press law. In his words, 'should the enemies of Islam, the revolution and the Islamic system take over or infiltrate the press, a great danger would threaten the security, unity and the faith of the people and, therefore, I cannot allow myself to keep quiet on this crucial issue'. He added, 'the current law, to a degree, has been able to prevent the appearance of this great calamity, and its interpretation and similar actions that have been anticipated by the parliamentary committee are not legitimate and not in the interest of the country and the system'.[31]

Khatami's second term in office continued to be punctuated with mass closures of pro-reform publications and efforts to stifle the reformist activism. In fact, the judiciary closed the pro-reform daily *Hambastegi* on 8 August 2001, the very day Khatami took his oath of office.[32] The Press Court, the Special Court for the Clergy, and the Revolutionary Courts proceeded to crack down on nearly every reformist newspaper. The closure of these publications dealt a serious blow to the reform movement as it blocked the reformists' main channel for communicating their message to the public. The second half of the reformist presidency saw even more barriers established against the symbols of reformism. Hard-line conservatives not only closed newspapers, they fined or imprisoned those who talked with the foreign media or participated in western conferences, and harassed human rights activists and lawyers. Reformist *Majles* deputies, among them women, were prosecuted by the judiciary for criticising conservatives in parliamentary discussions. Fatemeh Haghighatjoo, a prominent member of the women's lobby in the parliament, called for prosecution of the Judiciary Speaker for accusing parliament of 'running an inquisition' during the election of jurists to the Guardian Council.[33] She was sentenced to 22 months in prison for offending Islamic principles and defaming the Guardian Council.[34] Later, this analysis will explain why the radicals' defensive and sometimes aggressive posture was very much a product of insecurity vis-à-vis Khatami's political programme, which they feared was aimed at uprooting their position.

On 10 June 2003, student demonstrations broke out in Tehran. What began as a protest at the University of Tehran, against the regime's intention to privatise university studies and charge tuition, quickly broadened, spreading across Iran and lasting for ten days. Protest against conservative regime heads and calls for democracy were voiced during the demonstrations, as were demands for Khatami's resignation.[35] Prosecutor General Ayatollah Abdol Al-Nabi Namazi announced that the regime had jailed 4,000 people.[36] Nevertheless, reformists downplayed the incident, citing the demonstrations as proof that the regime was free and democratic. Khatami stated: 'what differentiates democratic from non-democratic societies is the existence of demonstrations of this kind'.[37] Foreign Ministry spokesman, Hamid Reza Assefi, added, 'It is natural that in a democratic country students call for their demands to be materialised. We are proud that we are living in a democratic country that derives its mandate from the people'.[38]

Opposition and Khatami's Second Presidential Bid

Khatami's second election differed vastly from the 1997 election. First, it was far more muddled. The 1997 election – despite Khatami's unexpected victory – offered Iranian voters a clear picture of the competition well before voting day. Although the Guardian Council approved the four presidential candidates only a month before the election, the four candidates had declared their intent to run long before their eligibility was announced. As a result, their different platforms and political affiliations became widely known. In his second presidential bid, in contrast, Khatami did not declare his intention of running until two days before the registration deadline. There was rampant speculation about the list of candidates until the Guardian Council announced the slate of approved candidates just three weeks before the day of the election. Unlike the 1997 election, campaign platforms were relegated to the back seat, and issues such as Khatami's decision to run and the future of political reform were the central focus.

The 2001 presidential race did not generate the same level of enthusiasm about political reform as did the 1997 elections. In 1997, voters had the hope that Khatami's election would pave the way for transformation. In the weeks before the 1997 election, it became apparent that every vote would count, and excitement replaced the apathy that had plagued past presidential elections. As already remarked upon, the surprisingly massive and enthusiastic voter turnout helped launch not only a very popular presidency but also a dynamic reform movement. By 2001, this had given way to a prevailing public mood of great disillusionment, and of great indifference towards the incumbent candidate.

The onslaught of anti-reform tactics had placed Khatami in a difficult and delicate position. Every time a newspaper was shut down, or a political rally or meeting disrupted, or an ally arrested on fabricated charges, Khatami's inability to condemn or counter the act (beyond expressing his regret) was progressively exposed. The impact of these events was cumulative, day by day, revealing the unfavourable balance of power and the reformists' inability to initiate practical change. Markedly unwilling to enter into open confrontation, Khatami did little to challenge the situation. His passive nature and his call for a gradual, evolutionary approach to change placed him at odds with some of his own supporters who demanded more assertiveness. Many supporters believed that Khatami had reached a political dead end in Iranian politics. Openly embarrassed about his powerlessness, Khatami was hesitant to run for a second term unless he could be assured of a less hindered presidency.[39] However, these reservations ultimately gave way to a practical political assessment: inasmuch as he was the single most visible symbol (if not icon) of the reform movement, a decision not to run would have signalled in no uncertain terms the movement's defeat. Once Khatami finally decided to run, he kept it a secret. In choosing to keep his opponents in the dark until the last possible moment, he offered them less time to react to his candidacy. Moreover, when he actually did announce his decision he focused less on his platform than he had four years earlier, choosing instead to throw light on practical concerns and problems. He did not present himself as an eager candidate, admitting that 'many have suffered, and there is still a risk that others will be abandoned to their fates'.[40] Initially, there had been no fewer than 800 other candidates seeking the presidency before the Guardian Council narrowed the field to ten, leaving Khatami as the sole 'moderate' candidate. All of the other contenders had ties to conservative parties, and two of the leading candidates, Defence Minister Shamkhani and former Minister of Intelligence, Ali Fallahian, had strong ties to the military. The conservatives, however, failed to put forwards a candidate of their own and did not officially back any of Khatami's rivals.

On 8 June 2001, Khatami won by a landslide, securing nearly 80 per cent of the popular vote. Whereas four-fifths of the 43 million eligible voters turned out, the overall turnout was smaller – 33 per cent of the electorate did not vote in 2001, compared with 18 per cent that did not vote in 1997. Clearly, the political gridlock had deflated expectations, leading a segment of the electorate to trade its patience for indifference. Although second-term presidential elections had previously drawn relatively low voter turnouts (as did the re-elections of Khamenei in 1985 and Rafsanjani in 1993), the lower turnout in this instance reflected the massive disillusionment after the high expectations of the past four years. All the same, Khatami won the election by a huge margin: Khatami took 21.7 million votes, 76 per cent of the 28.2 million votes cast, surpassing the 20 million that he won in 1997.[41] His nearest rival, Ahmad Tavakoli, the candidate favoured by the conservative clerical establishment, secured 4.4 million votes.[42]

The landslide victory furnished a much-needed boost to the reform movement. It was a statement that while demands for a civil society had not fully materialised, the electorate was not disheartened. Khatami's re-election was a sign that the vast majority of Iran's electorate believed it still had both a stake in the electoral system and some hope for reform. Nevertheless, the conservatives showed little sign of yielding, despite their overwhelming defeat, and continued to use the organisations they controlled to place added pressure on the reformers.

Remarkably, the power struggle reared its head at Khatami's inauguration, in an ominous start to his second term. According to the constitution, the inaugural ceremony could not be held without the presence of all members of the Guardian Council. The reformist-dominated parliament had refused to approve the Guardian Council's nominees proposed by head of the judiciary, Ayatollah Shahroudi. They claimed that the nominees were politically biased and lacked the requisite legal training.[43] Khamenei intervened and postponed the inauguration until the issue was resolved. In a meeting attended by Khatami, Rafsanjani, Mehdi Karroubi and Guardian Council representatives, the Expediency Discernment Council decided on a 'parliamentary bypass mechanism'. This mechanism would reshuffle Shahroudi's nominees before parliament in a set of rounds requiring a progressively diminished number of votes for approval. Thus, in the second round of voting, two of the nominees were approved by a majority of just over sixty votes. Some 70 per cent of the *Majles* deputies (166) cast blank ballots in an organised protest, accusing Shahroudi of 'failure to cooperate with them in approving the list'.[44] Some deputies actually walked out in protest during Shahroudi's speech given at the swearing-in ceremony. The president's brother, deputy *Majles* Speaker, Mohammad Reza Khatami, protested against the Expediency Discernment Council's bias in favour of the judiciary, and argued that the *Majles* 'does not agree with the Council's decision but has no other alternative'.[45] The charade finally ended when the Expediency Discernment Council sided with the judiciary and forced the appointment of conservatives. The dispute's resolution meant that Khatami was inaugurated three days later than originally scheduled. The reformist daily *Iran News* issued a rather alarmist article warning that if the disputes between the *Majles* and the judiciary continued, intervention by the

Expediency Discernment Council 'was likely to replace parliament as the legislative body'.[46]

The whole affair exposed the president's relative lack of power in the political organism. In his inaugural speech, Khatami acknowledged the previous years' setbacks for the reform movement, but he tried to stay above the political fray: 'I will not paint my critics and opponents as those opposed to Islam, the revolution, freedom, or people', the president said, 'but will value their lawful presence, and will respect them and avoid insulting their dignity'. He vowed to enact reforms demanded by his supporters and warned that failure would reflect badly on the very idea of Islamic government.[47]

After his inauguration, Khatami presented his government. However, the re-elected president was once again caught between the hammer – conservatives who effectively ruled the country – and the anvil – a reformist parliament calling for more reform-orientated cabinet nominees. Khatami presented a government fundamentally similar to the previous one. The rightist ministers (Minister of Defence, Ali Shamkhani, who had run against Khatami in the presidential election; Minister of Justice, Mohammad Shoushtari; Minister of Foreign Affairs, Kharazi; Minister of Intelligence, Ali Younesi; and Minister of the Interior, Abdolvahed Moussavi-Lari) all kept their seats, despite the reformists' demands in parliament to replace them. There were, however, five new nominees, with most changes concerning the interior portfolios. In general, both the reformist and the conservative press were sharply critical of Khatami's timidity in his ministerial nominations, particularly as the economy was showing signs of distress (the nominees to economic posts were said to be not sufficiently qualified or experienced).[48] Despite threats by both conservative and reformist members of the *Majles*, all of Khatami's cabinet nominees were approved.

2004 Majles Elections

On 20 February 2004, Iran elected the Seventh *Majles*. The election was widely criticised by both Iranian and international observers for the heavy-handed manner in which the conservative Guardian Council had intervened in the electoral process. This super-body disqualified an estimated 44 per cent of the candidates (3533 out of 8145) from standing for the election – by some counts almost four times the number of barred candidates in the 2000 *Majles* elections.[49] Among those initially disqualified were several prominent reformist politicians including many incumbents. As a result, the conservative factions recaptured control of the *Majles* at the expense of the reformist coalition. Altogether, over 80 incumbents were barred from participating, including the leader of the reformist party, the IIPF and Mohammad Reza Khatami, as well as Behzad Nabavi, Mohsen Mirdamadi and Mohsen Armin. These moderates had served on some of the most important *Majles* committees, including Foreign Affairs, National Security and Judicial Affairs, and their disqualification marked one of the most significant setbacks for the Second of Khordad Movement.

The announcement of the disqualifications provoked outrage among the reformers, who accused their conservative rivals of trying to steal the vote. A sit-in was staged by 140 legislators who threatened to boycott the election. The sit-in was followed by all of the provincial governors (in charge of the organisation of the elections around the country), and a few members of the presidential cabinet, warning that they might resign. Several ministers submitted letters of resignation as a sign of protest. The Guardian Council, at the request of the Supreme Leader, backed off slightly by reinstating 200 candidates and announcing that more reinstatements would follow.

Voter turnout for the 2004 parliamentary elections was low, once again demonstrating public apathy in response to political infighting. The Ministry of Interior, responsible for the mechanics of the elections, claimed that half of all eligible voters participated, while western sources pegged the figure at around 30 per cent. Around 51 per cent of eligible voters (23,725,724 out of 46,351,032) reportedly cast their ballots, which was meagre compared with the 69 per cent voter turnout four years earlier. Factored into this percentage is the participation of conscripts, civil servants and those dependent upon the state.[50] Moreover, almost 1.4 million people, about six per cent of the voters, indicated their dissent by casting a spoiled or voided ballot. The acutely reduced turnout was a statement – or, more appropriately, an unmistakably dramatic reaction – to the disqualification of candidates. Voter inaction, moreover, was a loud vote of no-confidence for conservative institutions such as the Guardian Council. The conservative victory in the Seventh *Majles* did not actually represent a radical departure in the conduct of politics in Iran. Their institutional upper hand in the power struggle persisted, just as it had since the beginning of Khatami's first presidential victory, and even when the reformists held a majority in the Sixth *Majles*. Remarkably, Khatami was now both the president of the country and the leader of the opposition.

Failure to Bridge the Political Divide

It has already been established that the most serious hurdle encountered by the Second of Khordad Front was institutional constraint. The limited powers of the president, and the counter-attack waged by conservative institutions that did not favour social or political transformation, created an impasse that deprived the movement of the dynamism and spirit it required to bring about substantive change. The pathology of this impasse can be traced to the essence, theory and practical application of *eslahat* (reform). One important criticism can be levelled against the reformists concerning this matter. In describing this shortcoming, the groundwork must be established by saying a few words about the intellectual debates circulating in Iran when Khatami came to power.

When Khatami campaigned for reform, he spoke of the importance of the rule of law, of civil society, intellectual space, the need to include all Iranians in the political decision-making process and the need for a global discourse. His political platform can be regarded as the political edge of a deep socio-cultural movement for *Shi'i* reformation well under way by the 1990s. In Iran, there had emerged a reformist discourse that spoke of 'religious democracy', 'pluralism', 'civil society', 'citizenship', and addressed the principles of modernity, pre-modernity and post-modernity. The debate took place between both sides of the political spectrum. In the conservative camp, for example, was Reza Davari-Ardakani, who represented the Heideggerian 'anti-modern' traditionalist school of thought in the post-revolutionary era by adopting religious rhetoric against modernity. Lambasting what he perceived to be the imposed nature of modernity in Iran, Davari wrote:

> Modernity is a tree that was planted in the west and has spread everywhere. For many years we have been living under one of the dying and faded branches of this tree and its dried shadow, which is still hanging over our heads. Although we have taken refuge in Islam, the shadow of this branch has still not yet totally disappeared from over our heads. In fact, neither we nor it have left each other alone. What can be done with this dried branch?[51]

Davari maintained that the branches and the entire tree of modernity had to be eradicated through the formation of a distinctive intellect – one that was distinguishable from the western intellectual model. Davari perceived the western notion of democracy, based on a separation of politics and religion, as decadent. Instead, he advocated a society grounded in the axioms of guardianship and prophethood.[52] Thus, to root out the tree of modernity, Davari recommended humanity to pledge with God rather than pledge with the 'self', which he perceived to be the pernicious core of modernity. He claimed that western civilisation was declining because of the effects of alienation, or what Emile Durkheim referred to in *Suicide* as 'anomie'. Davari maintained that the solution for the secular and materialistic west was religion and divine inspiration.[53] Furthermore, Davari reminded Iranian intellectuals that the west had to be perceived as a unified whole, and an essence from which the non-western world could not pick and choose.

On the other side of the argument was leading reformist intellectual, Abdolkarim Soroush, a British-educated philosopher of science who in the 1990s lectured extensively in Iran and abroad about the need for Islamic reformism. Soroush was an outspoken critic of Davari's conservative views, which, he argued, left no room for constructive dialogue. Davari, he maintained, was coercing people to accept or to reject the west. He argued that the west did not constitute a totality and that what came from the west was not necessarily 'contaminating'. Soroush considered democracy and human rights to be universal concepts, thereby rejecting their western origin and arguing that they were central to Iranian culture. Soroush believed that Iranians were the heirs to three cultures: pre-Islamic Persian, Islamic and western. Instead of privileging one over the other, he maintained that Iranians needed to reconcile all three.

Unlike Davari, Soroush advocated cultural exchange. Soroush spoke of the hindrances caused by dogmatism and instead promoted mutual recognition: 'I do not believe that a religious government like the Islamic Republic of Iran has the intention of converting the whole world to Islam and Islamic government. The first step should be to promote and respect religious thought around the world'.[54] Islamic reform required that Iranians move beyond the westernisation label and select aspects of western culture that would benefit Iranian culture. According to Soroush, such a free and optional approach to the west would not lead to blind imitation of its culture; however, if denied the chance to make a choice the country would succumb to westernisation.[55]

In 1992, Soroush made the contention that Islam had to be treated as a religion rather than a revolutionary ideology. Soroush stated that Islam – the religion rather than the ideology – was subject to change, depending on contextual factors and interpretation.[56] Soroush parted from the typical Islamic modernists by adopting the 'hermeneutic approach', a methodology that would allow multiple interpretations of Islamic texts. In a 1997 article entitled *Siratha-yi Mustaquim* ('Straight Paths'), Soroush advanced the notion of religious pluralism by relying less on Islamic jurisprudence as the basis for law (as was typical of Islamic modernists), and by drawing heavily on the tradition of Islamic mysticism. In this work, he noted that accepting cultural and religious pluralism necessitated the importance of social pluralism. He made the case that 'a pluralistic society is a non-ideological society, that is, [a society] without an official interpretation and [official] interpreters, and founded on pluralist reason'.[57] In fact, Soroush made the controversial argument that in the modern world the state should seek solutions to social issues in social science and in the religious values of society and not exclusively in Islamic jurisprudence.

These were indeed controversial but important debates that were circulating throughout society. However, most of these discourses were heavily theoretical and philosophical in nature, and mostly restricted to the milieu of the intellectual elite. Indeed, to many these debates were beyond comprehension in practical terms. Consider Dariush Ashuri's contention that 'the future of Iran depended on this movement of religious enlightenment, which was capable of bringing about a synthesis between tradition and traditional thought and the heritage of the modern world'.[58] What did this mean in practical terms and how would this apply to an Iranian context? It is important to recognise that when conservatives, hard-liners or traditionalists are discussed, it is with reference to Islamist ideologues, to the clerical body, to martyr's foundations, to Islamic associations, revolutionary organisations and committees, and Islamic militias and security forces. These highly religious, ideological entities felt they were entrusted with the mission of ensuring that the religiousness of the regime remained intact. (Naturally, as in any regime, some intentions were less noble and geared more towards securing power.) This group typically feared the possibility of west-toxication, and of western secular, liberal influences. For these groups, survival of the theological underpinnings of the Islamic Republic was cardinal.

Thus, when reformists spoke of democratisation, pluralism and civil society, concepts that were thrown around in slogans, speeches and publications, the conservatives became anxious. The question was: did these concepts mean the same thing in the secular, liberal western societies? What did 'social participation' mean in a post-revolutionary Islamic theocracy? There was no doubt that Iran needed to place itself on the path of reform, for the many reasons elaborated earlier. An Islamic modernity, eventuated 'from below', with the blessing of a popular mandate, was just what Iran needed – to keep the youth at bay; to respond to society's needs; to initiate a civilisational upgrade – to push the Islamic Republic into the twenty-first century. In principle, this was precisely what Iran needed at the juncture at which it found itself in 1997. Nevertheless, such vast social engineering and transformation needed years of preparation, and of consultation and debate in order to reconcile society's disparate groups before it could be implemented. A charismatic leader, even with attractive slogans and an electoral victory, was not enough to affect substantive change in a country in which the political machinery was in the hands of those very groups that feared change in a fragile republic that had fought tooth and nail to preserve its integrity.

With hindsight, which is always an unfair advantage, it would have been useful if the reformist camp had fully elaborated on what these slogans entailed – in practical, day-to-day terms. How would these theories and slogans be translated into practical use? What were the boundaries between state and society and religious institutions? What institutional form would pluralism take in the Islamic Republic? These questions needed to be addressed explicitly, and each concept needed to be articulated with reference to their application in the Iranian theocracy. Democracy cannot be quantified, but it can be defined. Khatami needed to present a clear and precise definition of what an Islamic, religious democracy entailed. He and his supporters needed to elaborate on concepts of democracy, civil society, pluralism and *gofteh-guh* (dialogue), so that society would have an idea of what was permitted and what was not. Had Khatami initiated a robust internal dialogue on notions of religious democracy, civil society and Islamic modernity, amongst divergent segments of society and amongst the political elite, it is far more likely that conservative traditionalists would have been relatively more receptive to change. Would *eslahat* protect the interests of those who had fought to defend the revolution – those who felt they were entitled to have more influence in the Iranian social, political organism? Would their interests be preserved? Were they being discriminated against? These were real questions and issues that Khatami overlooked. Thus, it is not surprising that the more hard-line, radical elements of the conservative camp would use any means possible to preserve the status quo.

Furthermore, clear articulation of the slogans of *eslahat* would have protected the segments of society that had voted for Khatami, as it would have given them a clear picture of the restrictions on political life in society after he was nominated. In this way, Khatami would have protected students and intellectuals by giving them a realistic idea of the confines of democracy within the existing structure. Here was a president who had won on a democratic platform, and naturally his supporters would immediately assume that certain democratic practices would be tolerated under his leadership. Khatami was sending out a mixed message: on the one hand he was calling for democratic change, and he was pushing society in that direction; but then he would suddenly pull back by, for example, acting passively, as he was accused of doing during the student demonstrations. By definition – the western definition – civil society does not preclude demonstrations or protests, and the message Khatami sent out to his supporters when he reiterated support for civil society was that these practices were not banned outright. It became clear, however, that in the Islamic Republic these practices were unacceptable and in fact were prone to generating conflict amongst disparate groups. The crucial observation here is that concepts and practices needed to be delineated exhaustively and comprehensively, well ahead of time.

Khatami: Reformist or Conformist?

The political crises discussed above seriously tarnished Khatami's image as an effective, responsive leader. In December 2004, at the University of Tehran, students gave the embattled Khatami an angry and humiliating reception. He was bombarded with heckling and angry slogans reflecting widespread frustration with his failure to bring substantive liberal reforms to the country. Students chanted: 'Khatami, Khatami shame on you'; 'Khatami, we detest you'; 'Khatami, our votes were wasted on you' and 'where are your promised freedoms?'[59] Increasingly, students and intellectuals began to lose hope in Khatami, accusing him of being too passive in the face of the conservative onslaught.

Indeed, President Khatami demonstrated a certain passivity that was unusual for a president that had garnered over 70 per cent of the country's vote. For instance, he shifted his tone by condemning pro-democracy demonstrations, and by urging the youth to avoid provoking hard-liners. Another example stands out: Khatami reiterated often his bid to improve ties between Iran and the United States. He then went on to support the Supreme Leader's declaration that the arrival of US aid for the Bam earthquake should not be viewed as a harbinger of improving relations. This retreat was also evident in a harshly worded sermon claiming the United States was an enslaver of Iran.

Khatami was not passive, he was cautious, and to understand this it is necessary to put the reform movement in perspective. During the reformist presidency, the country was bursting with youth who were yearning for democratic change. At the same time, the institutional legal system of the Islamic Republic was in the hands of a powerful and deeply entrenched conservative theocracy that was reluctant to concede to popular will. This force not only controlled the important power centres of the country, but also had at its disposal the security apparatus and the loyalty of radical vigilante groups. In view of this resistance Khatami proposed 'managed change', which he believed would gradually ease the country into democratisation; however, the conservative oligarchy was unwilling to cooperate with the president and his mandate. Khatami tested the waters upon taking office and came to recognise that the situation could quickly become explosive; something as simple as an organised protest could lead to bloodshed. He explained this situation in his speech at the University of Tehran, suggesting that reforms had failed because he had bowed to the will of the Supreme Leader to avoid riots and to preserve stability.

As discussed above, the Iranian clerical establishment was simply not prepared to accept protests or demonstrations – however, this was not because they rejected democratic practices and procedures. Their defensiveness was largely guided by suspicion that reforms would compromise the stability and security of the regime, and jeopardise the hard-won gains of the revolution. As also mentioned above, this reaction was very much a conditioned response to what traditional elements of state and society viewed as a betrayal of revolutionary purism. Khatami could have allayed conservative anxiety by being more explicit about what a new political space would look like in an Islamic theocracy.

Kamran Giti provides an interesting profile of the reformist president: 'Khatami was not a general, not a 'philosopher king', in no way like a Marcus Aurelius. That ancient Roman emperor, during the day, killed people on the battlefield as an able, vicious, brutal general, in pursuit of the empire's greed for land; only at night did he write philosophical treaties on stoicism, grieving over the human condition'. Giti maintains that 'Khatami is a man who has grieved full time. He has refuted the old saying that "peace needs two sides; for war one will suffice". He managed to dodge a war of attrition'.[60] Indeed, Khatami can be credited with preventing a serious showdown during a very explosive period in Iran's modern history. There were scuffles in the *Majles* and disturbances on the street, but Khatami kept both his supporters and opponents at bay.

There were occasions, however, when Khatami and his allies demonstrated more assertiveness and risked incurring the disapproval of the Supreme Leader. For example, in January 1999, Khatami stunned the nation by forcing the exposure of the Ministry of Intelligence high officials' alleged involvement in the assassinations of dissident intellectuals and their attempt to mastermind a wave of political and cultural repression.[61] Another example was Khatami's reaction to the Guardian Council's disqualification of candidates to the 2004 *Majles*. He and his reformist allies bluntly told hard-liners to allow free and fair polls, and threatened to leave office en masse unless the conservatives rescinded their blacklist.

An even more significant show of assertiveness was the proposal for the 'twin bills'. In 2002, Khatami attempted to fight back with the submission of two pieces of legislation known collectively as the 'twin bills'. He argued that 'although the President is responsible for implementing the constitution, he, however, does not possess the minimum possibilities afforded to the presidency by the constitution'. Khatami continued, saying, 'for that reason, I will prepare a bill and present it to *Majles* soon, so that God willing, I will be able to perform the duty that is inside the constitution, religion, and the wish of the people, and that the people expect, with more authority and to a greater degree'.[62] Khatami described a bill to reform the election law, which was introduced to the Sixth *Majles* on 1 September 2002 by Vice President of Legal and Parliamentary Affairs, Mohammad Ali Abtahi. Its objective was to eliminate or at least reduce the Guardian Council's power to indiscriminately disqualify candidates from running for office. On 24 September, Abtahi submitted the second bill, which would enhance presidential authority. The bill would provide the president with the right to warn and even punish officials in the executive, legislative and judicial branches. It would also empower a committee of experts chosen by the legislature, the executive and the judiciary to overrule court verdicts. Khatami was even bold enough to ask for power to investigate constitutional violations by bodies that were normally answerable only to the Supreme Leader.[63] After a long struggle, the twin bills were rejected by the Guardian Council, which cited violations to the constitution and Islamic law. The two pieces of proposed legislation would have introduced small but key changes to the national election laws of Iran. Moreover, the legislation clearly defined the president's power to prevent constitutional violations by state institutions. Khatami himself described the twin bills as central to reform in Iran.

Indeed, to many observers Khatami embodied a curious amalgam of reformist and conformist tendencies. Throughout his presidency, the reformist leader pushed for change, but at the same time his tenure was punctuated by periods of stagnation, conservatism and inertia. This paradox was also reflected in his calls for a 'religious democracy'. This was a political blueprint reformist intellectuals and some *Shi'i* clerics were convinced was a viable political template for Iranian politics in the twenty-first century; their interpretations of sacred texts and the *sharia* were, of course, at odds with the doctrinaire reading furnished by obscurantist elements of the clerical establishment. The dispute over the orientation that Iran would follow in its development was won by the conservatives, who had the institutional might to set Iran on the trajectory they deemed suitable, even if it went against the popular mandate. As illustrated above, the turbulence in Iranian politics during the reform period was to a large extent the result of Iran's complex political system, rather than the essential unfeasibility of a 'religious democracy', or flaws in Khatami's character, or in his intentions.

Some have caricatured this famous cleric of moderate reputation as 'Ayatollah Gorbachev'. This is an interesting comparison as it allows some insights to be examined concerning Khatami's character. Indeed, Khatami represented a curious paradox: a theologian cloaked in Islamic garb, advancing a liberal social agenda. He was a contradictory figure, as was the reform blueprint he envisioned for Iran. The very essence of Khatami's political programme was the attempt to reconcile the traditional and the modern. His vision was conceived to transcend traditional ideological and sociological divisions and to lead the country on to a balanced developmental path. The goal was to transcend the dichotomy between conforming to native traditions and encouraging integration into the international community.

Khatami himself strongly personified the reconciliation of these divergent orientations. On one level, he had no difficulty in granting that the fundamentals of Iran's Islamic system were to remain, above anything else. He adamantly expressed this in an interview, stating that he believed in living his Islamic faith through social activism. In his own words, 'I still consider myself a humble and indeed insignificant member of my great nation who has not been able to contribute as much as the martyrs for the country'. Yet, on another level, it is also abundantly obvious that Khatami was not a typical mullah. While he was bearded, he was carefully barbered and robed in bespoke fashion. He regularly read western newspapers and magazines, had lived abroad, spoke German and English, and had written extensively on the topic of reconciling Islam to the modern world. Khatami ran a western-style presidential campaign, touring around the country giving interviews, and speaking with young people and women about his hobbies (working out, swimming and reading) and his favourite philosophers.

So, let us address a tentative answer to the question of whether Khatami was an Iranian Gorbachev. The evidence gathered must be sensitive to the larger picture wherein the two reformists obviously share deep similarities, as well as there being stark contrasts between them. Like Gorbachev, Khatami was the leader of a country undergoing major transformation, assuming the limelight in being the chief advocate of change to the status quo. Like Gorbachev, who had wanted to restructure the Soviet system without touching the socialist foundations (state ownership, the Communist Party's leading role and the regime's socialist goals), Khatami also wanted to introduce reforms without inducing any change to the regime's Islamic character. Similar to Gorbachev, the result of Khatami's moderate approach was a fundamental alteration in the character of international relations – the *Dialogue Among Civilisations* can be compared with Gorbachev's foreign policy framework, *Novoe Politicheskoe Myshlenie* (New Political Thinking). Moreover, just as Gorbachev battled to create a socialist society with a human face, Khatami struggled to inject the role of human agency and freedom into Iranian politics by fostering notions of pluralism, civil society and economic liberalism.

The overriding difference between the two is that Gorbachev began a process of restructuring and democratisation over which he lost control. This was not the case under Khatami, who combined active lobbying for civil society with passiveness in the face of radical forms of social protest. Khatami was a gradualist who, during various public demonstrations, demonstrated a marked inertia. What is more, Gorbachev had vast power, even though he himself was unwilling to oppose the communist conservatives. In contrast, Khatami was acutely hindered by the political structure and the limits to his presidential power. The culmination of perestroika (Gorbachev's programme for economic restructuring), despite Gorbachev's intentions, was the disintegration of the communist system. Gorbachev remains in the mind of his compatriots a tragic figure whom some will deify and others hate; some see him as a great reformer, others as a perfidious destroyer. Khatami left no such romanticised legacy. At worst, he was an ineffectual reformer and, at best, a visionary of change.

In this chapter, two key points have been explored. The first highlights the structural obstacles that Khatami encountered during his presidency. Khatami's presidency was a case where individual leadership was unable to stamp its preferences on a period, mainly because of constraints particular to Iran's political structure. According to a famous statement made by Khatami, his government survived on average one national crisis every nine days during his term of office. This underscores an important consideration: Khatami's reform movement cannot be regarded as a wholesale failure, but rather as a hampered effort weighed down by power structures – specifically, a conservative-leaning, veto-wielding Supreme Leader, influential unelected bodies that wanted to preserve the status quo, and inflexible radicals who were firmly committed to their revolutionary ideological vision. However, while

Khatami did make a genuine effort to initiate legal-constitutional changes such as the 'twin bills', he failed to sufficiently address the deep-rooted, almost phobic anxiety of the conservatives vis-à-vis the western aspects of *eslahat.* As detailed here, Khatami could have done much more to allay the fears of the traditional segments of society who feared the possibility of 'west-toxication' and the infiltration of western influences. Khatami called for a dialogue among civilisations but that dialogue had to begin inside Iran.

The second observation made here is that the Iranian polity made its voice heard by protesting against the Guardian Council's *Majles* disqualifications, by staging sit-ins, submitting letters of resignation and by not voting. This 'non-action' is not a sign of political defeat but of defiance and non-compliance. Indeed, Khatami fell short of consolidating the democratic practices and procedures he had promised. Yet, for the first time since the revolution, a greater sense of civic assertiveness in political affairs was seen – a development that was clearly attributable to Khatami's efforts.

7

KHATAMI'S REVOLUTION AND BEYOND

Khatami's popular reform movement was one of the most ambitious attempts at social engineering since the days of the revolution. Armed with a popular mandate, the reformist current launched the great experiment of *eslahtalabi* (reformism). This ideology advocated civil society, the rule of law, economic integration with the world and political rapprochement. In practice, of course, these ideals were tempered by the challenges of trying to consolidate a 'religious democracy' in a conservative theocracy, as well as the inherent shortcomings in Khatami's approach to implementing substantive change. As seen earlier, the views of politically engaged Iranians constituted a broad political spectrum. These divergent political ideologies manifested themselves in different political factions whose defensive strategies and tactics constituted a severe and dynamic power struggle during Khatami's years in office. Every faction at each point of the political spectrum had some consequential effect on the reform movement. This chapter will re-examine their ideologies and philosophies in order to draw a few general insights about the scope, shortcomings and achievements of Khatami's reform movement. The chapter will also draw attention to evidence suggesting that Iranian reformism continued to prevail even under the conservative presidency of Mahmoud Ahmadinejad. As we shall explain, the legacy of the Khatami experiment was a budding pluralistic momentum that prevailed well beyond the end of his eight-year presidency.

Khatami's Conceptual Revolution

Since the election of Khatami in 1997, intense political and philosophical debate has resulted in conflicting notions of what the Islamic Republic should look like. At one end of the political spectrum was the radical right, which embraced an absolutist position. Concerned with preserving the *ummah* (the collective Islamic community), the radical right placed little emphasis on the individual's domain of privacy or the role of the individual in state affairs. This ideological position favoured a centralised state that exercised control in all areas. The state was to be governed under the absolute rule of the Supreme Leader, who was seen as the representative of divine will on earth. The radical right did not appear to place much emphasis on the democratic aspects of the post-revolution constitution. For instance, they did not see the source of legitimacy of the president's office in the popular mandate, but in the subsequent appointment of the president by the Supreme Leader. They scorned anyone that challenged the absolute power of the Supreme Leader and were suspicious of the notion of civil society. As has been demonstrated here, this faction held a monopolistic view, excluding any compromise on the issue of clerical control over all aspects of politics and society. To this end, the conservative bloc used a variety of tactics in combating reformist forces.

The conservative right was made up of clerics, the economic mainstay of the bazaar and the 'cultural conservatives' (who concerned themselves mainly with cultural and moral policies rather than economics). This faction shared most of the cultural and political views of the radical right, but believed in a populist authoritarian system (as opposed to absolutism), which allowed for a limited space of individual privacy and free-market policies. During Khatami's presidency this bloc controlled the main levers of power and regularly used its position to dampen the reform current. Since the presidential 2005 victory of the far right, however, this bloc has started to emphasise the role of popular will.

Further along the ideological spectrum was the modern right – the technocrats who placed more emphasis on economic reconstruction than on political or cultural reform. Although many technocrats were very traditional they still strove to establish a modern industrial economy, which entailed higher taxation, foreign borrowing and investment, and the kind of structural changes that were inspired by the World Bank. The pro-Rafsanjanites adopted a relatively liberal attitude towards social policies, and articulated the need for a more dynamic *velayat-e faqih*. This bloc was compatible with the left of the spectrum – the proponents of the reform movement. The reformists were advocating Islamic reformism, which accentuated the importance of the reinterpretation of sacred Islamic texts. Unlike the radical right and conservative or traditional right, the reformists and some pragmatic technocrats concentrated on the republican aspects of the regime.

From Islamic Revolution to Islamic Reformism

It is crucial at this point to begin to see that this variegated political spectrum is generally relevant to the project of reform in a broader context. The twentieth century saw an epic struggle for the modern world. The forces of western liberalism, combining rationalism, secularism and individualism challenged the European alternatives of dynastic absolutism, extremist nationalism and Marxism-Leninism. With the collapse of the Soviet Union, Eastern Europe was 'westernised' and what Francis Fukuyama called the 'liberal idea' – the combination of the rule of law, liberal democracy and market capitalism – emerged as the basis of the global order. Liberalism transcended and was exported beyond the borders of Europe and North America, and became by far the most important model of what the future would look like. Simon Murden advances this notion by arguing that liberalism became 'the dominant value system of a new global hegemony'.[1]

Non-western societies that were less familiar with secularism and pluralism found it difficult to adapt. One such and perhaps even a paradigmatic case was Mohammad Reza Shah Pahlavi, the autocratic moderniser of Iran. The rapid tempo of globalisation in the late twentieth century triggered a multitude of reactions. Cultural imitation and synthesis were commonplace, but so were more regressive reactions. Religious revivalism was a reaction to the west's hegemony because religious faith was so irrelevant to its ideas and practices. The reaction to 'west-toxication' was manifested in a great cultural and religious reawakening. Ordinary

Muslims reaffirmed Muslim rituals and social practices, and Muslim intellectuals turned away from overtly European and western thought and towards Islamic references. The more traditional elements of the Islamic revival scorned modernity's secularism, individualism and perceived moral emptiness. The Islamic revolutionaries of 1978–9 reacted against the western liberal model by institutionalising the idea of an Islamic state built on religio-political institutions, and guided by the *sharia*, and the moral and political prescriptions of the charismatic founder of the Islamic Republic, Ayatollah Khomeini.

The reality, however, was that neither Iranian society nor the state were an island immune to the effects of globalised modernity. Iran needed to become involved in and adapt to the processes of global unification, market expansion and scientific and technological cooperation. A number of powerful political, economic and sociological forces highlighted the need to institutionalise change and ease the country out of isolation. These included a burgeoning youth population; socially and politically conscious women; a cosmopolitan consumer culture; growing education rates; higher numbers of university registrants; a proliferation of philosophical discourses; calls for civil society; critical public opinion; the information age and isomorphic communication; and cultural diffusion. In other words, Iran was a society in transition.

This is not to suggest that Iran was headed for 'westernisation' or a cultural homogenisation of sorts, but rather integration and internationalisation; this required reform or even an upgrade of existing political institutions and practices. In short, Iran had no choice but to modernise itself. It has been shown here that both the radical right and the conservative right perceived globalisation and democratisation as a western assault on the theocracy. In April 2000, Khamenei conveyed this perception: 'What is globalisation? It means that a group of world powers, a number of countries – mainly those who have influence over the UN and mainly those countries that have been colonialists in the past – want to expand their culture, economy and traditions throughout the world'. In relation to economic globalisation, he contended, 'They want to make decisions. That is what globalisation means'.[2]

The conservative establishment – because of its fear of 'west-toxication' – tried to ignore the reality of globalisation and public opinion. It has been explained here that this deep-rooted conservative apprehension was symptomatic of a perceived western cultural onslaught, for which Khatami offered little consolation. His remedy was an Islamic-Iranian path to modernity in the form of a fully-fledged religious democracy. What is relevant here is that the developmental path that Khatami envisioned for Iran was unique. It was a home-grown developmental path, inspired 'from below' and derived from two resounding presidential victories and the subsequent mobilisation of reformist forces – students, intellectuals, women, politicians, technocrats and moderate clerics. This book is called *Khatami's Iran* because, in his presidency, modernity was the equivalent of the masses desire for change.

Iran is confronted with the same social and political realities under President Ahmadinejad. The predominantly conservative/traditionalist personalities who control the levers of power need to acknowledge that Iran's politically attentive public has grown significantly over the past decade and that it is essential to continue reforming the country in the face of increased popular appeals for socio-political modernisation. Furthermore, the leadership needs to respond dynamically to the forces of globalisation and to adapt the country to the twenty-first century. For this, more internal debate is essential in order to work out the practicalities and intricacies of establishing a genuinely modernised Islamic Republic. What can also help is a more open-minded and pragmatic reading of religious texts. The Qur'an itself is the most democratic of institutions for the very reason that it is open to diverse interpretations. In fact, the Qur'an reiterates that it is eternally truthful; thus, it is not limited to seventh-century Medinan society, but applicable to the twenty-first century and beyond. This was the philosophy embraced by the *roshankefran* (enlightened intellectuals) who advanced the importance of more diverse interpretations and readings of sacred texts to support their cause. It is a strategy that can help any government of any orientation to give Iran the civilisational upgrade that it needs to usher it into the twenty-first century.

The contemporary debate on Islamic reform can be supported by many of the writings and sayings of the founder of the Islamic Republic, Ayatollah Khomeini. In fact, in the philosophical debates that emerged in 1997, many political factions routinely quoted the Ayatollah, particularly when there were contradictory positions taken by the leader on various subjects. His diverse discourses allowed ideologically disparate groups to appropriate those ideas that were compatible with their particular agenda and to ignore those that were incompatible. Of course, this task was easier for the conservatives, especially in relation to the issues concerning freedom and morality. At the same time, many of his declarations could be understood as compatible with the democratic principles embraced by the reformists. For example, the reformists and advocates of *mardom salari* frequently invoked Ayatollah Khomeini's statement that the position of the government vis-à-vis the people is that of a servant vis-à-vis its master.[3] Sussan Siavoshi has noted that such statements provided ready-made rhetorical devices for the reformist groups in their attempt to advance their campaign.[4]

Let it not be forgotten that Ayatollah Khomeini was the Islamic Republic's first reformer. Ervand Abrahamian explains that the Ayatollah was not an extremist – a label he associates with 'religious inflexibility, intellectual purity, political traditionalism, even social conservatism'. Instead, he perceives the founder of the Islamic Republic to be a populist, a term associated with 'ideological adaptability and intellectual flexibility'.[5] Siavoshi argues, 'the different dynamic of pre-revolutionary, revolutionary, and post-revolutionary events influenced his [Khomeini's] utterances, if not his beliefs'.[6] In the course of post-revolutionary development in particular, Ayatollah Khomeini modified many of his earlier suggestions regarding political structures. One concession – his insistence on the 'Islamic Republic of Iran' as opposed to 'Islamic Iran' – was clearly aimed at gaining approval from those who were concerned with the country's democratic/theocratic balance. Another example worth citing is the establishment of the Assembly of Experts. This congressional body performs the function of a regulatory agency and places checks and balances on the power of the Supreme Leader. The Assembly has the authority to nominate the Supreme Leader in the event that the incumbent is removed or dies. The Expediency Discernment Council was another body the Ayatollah created to ensure that the public's interest was protected. This council was given the authority to go against religious laws if the well-being of the community required it.[7]

Ayatollah Khomeini made many statements that were in accord with the reformists' agenda. Most of these declarations and sayings developed in response to unfolding events. For example, his encouragement of rational and enlightened discourse is captured in the following statement: 'A perfect human being is the one who, once s/he is convinced of the validity of her/his position, strives to assert her/his position through reasoning, because one cannot force one's opinion on others'.[8] Concerning human rights, he declared, 'There should be no verbal abuse of the incarcerated … Under the Islamic government no one has the right to deny food, or to slap, or to torture a prisoner'.[9] This statement was actually invoked by the reformists in the *Majles* to advance a bill to ban the torture of prisoners. It was finally approved by the Guardian Council in April 2004, after being rejected three times.[10] In relation to government accountability and transparency, Ayatollah Khomeini declared, 'Each and every member of [the] nation had the right to directly and publicly impeach and criticise. If he fails to do so, he has acted against his Islamic responsibility'.[11] He underlined the importance of government responsibility further: 'People who are in the rank of opposition are free to express their disagreements and the high clergy of towns, and villages, and the nation itself, have the responsibility to protect such freedom'.[12] These statements all had the potential to legitimise the reformist discourse, providing assurances to the radicals and conservatives that Islamic reformism in Iran would not involve deviation from the standards set by the leader of the revolution. The country would have then had the chance of becoming the standard-bearer of a twenty-first century Islamic republic. Had Khatami fostered a more extensive, critical and interactive intra-societal dialogue along these lines, *before* initiating his reform project, it is probable that conservative resistance would have been much less severe.

Khatamism

This study questions Karl Marx's famous tale that rejects the emphasis on the force of personality as a principal agent of social change and looks instead for an explanation in impersonal economic causes. This analysis highlights why an objective narrator of modern Iranian history must take into account the importance of the *leader* of the reformist movement. First, it can be said with some certainty that Khatami's personality embodied the very changes he sought to implement in the Islamic Republic. A president who embraced democratic values, but who was also staunchly dedicated to the revolutionary ideals of the theocracy, Khatami was a leader that cannot easily be typologised. A 'modernising mullah', Khatami embodied a unique contradiction in the region. He was both religious and enlightened: he was the son of a cleric and had a traditional upbringing; he was trained in Qom, the stronghold of Iran's conservative clergy. Yet, he was also influenced by some of the west's leading critical philosophers of enlightened rational thought, and he was inspired by the progressive economic and technological accomplishments of the west.

This dualism was inherent in his vision for Iran, a land he hoped would adapt to the calls for modernity while retaining its religious, cultural and civilisational identity. This political model was called a 'religious democracy' – a prototype he sought to implement through the exercise of 'modernisation from below'. Even visually, Khatami exemplified a paradox that defied monolithic classifications. Speaking about Khatami's visit to the United States in November 2006 for a series of lectures, journalist Robert Fisk made the following observation: 'Mr. Khatami might appear an improbable figure in the breakfast room of one of Chicago's smartest hotels, dressed in his black turban and long gown, his spectacles giving him the appearance of a university don'.[13] Indeed, Khatami broke many stereotypes and preconceptions of what a former executive of an Islamic republic would look like. Khatami aimed to dismantle these stereotypes by attempting to transform Iran into a modern-day democracy; albeit, a unique and distinctive democracy predicated on theological concepts. It is important to note that Khatami did not aim to relegate Islam to the official state religion as in typical secular democracies. Rather, Khatami aimed to accentuate the democratic aspects of the existing theocratic system.

Khatami was the agent of change, mobilising the masses with his message and populist presidential style. Very much like Ayatollah Khomeini, Khatami was a charismatic leader who spoke the lingua franca of the people. In fact, Khatami devoted enormous attention to cultivating relations with the public, evidenced by the president's unannounced visits to shops, schools, hospitals and food ration lines. In a report for the *New York Times*, Elaine Sciolino described Khatami's populist manoeuvrings: 'This is a man who went on public buses. He's the kind of baby-kissing politician we're used to here in the United States. He rolled up his sleeves and gave blood. He tries to straddle the world of Islam and Islamic clericalism, and the world of the people'.[14] Given his enthusiasm and proselytising style, Khatami came well-equipped for the challenge of breathing new life into the country. His populist strategy helped narrow the gulf between state and society and instilled in the populace the hope that they had some control over their destiny. Under Khatami, there was a veritable 'movement' based on a solid vision that attracted a broad social base.

One interesting concept that Khatami introduced into the political sphere was the concept of *akhlagh*. Khatami's former adviser, Mohammad Javad Faridzadeh, observes that this was one of the former president's most important contributions to Iranian politics.[15] *Akhlagh* in this context roughly translates into social adeptness, and refers to the finesse and etiquette required in social dealings and communications. Khatami's flair for diplomacy in the international realm and his 'people skills' were carried into the Iranian public sphere. The female *Majles* deputy, Fatemeh Haghighatjoo, reports that Khatami raised awareness about the negative cultural characteristics of Iranian society, and brought to the fore such concepts as patience, tolerance, dialogue, questioning and answering, mutual respect and democratic family relations. More broadly, she argues, he changed the traditional master/follower relationship and introduced aspects of a democratic culture.[16] Indeed, anecdotal evidence suggests that during Khatami's presidency, politicians, civil servants and bureaucrats became more mild-mannered, especially in dealing with women and young people. Haggardness and brutishness were replaced with refinement and respect. Revolutionary zeal in post-revolutionary Iran often manifested itself in the defensive posture of government administrators. With a docile president at the helm, the rest of the government structure followed suit, and this trickled down throughout society at large. This was the sort of dynamism that Khatami brought to Iran, a milestone achievement for the Iranian public.

Khatami demonstrated the importance of *akhlagh* in the post-presidency years. In the wake of the nuclear standoff, at a time when Iran faced the threat of sanctions and referral to the Security Council, Khatami travelled to the United States. He spoke at the Islamic Society of North America convention in Chicago, made a presentation at an inter-faith event at the Washington National Cathedral and attended a United Nations conference.[17] Why was it that Khatami was permitted to travel in the United States when, since 1979, the United States had barred Iranian dignitaries from stepping outside a 25-mile radius of the United Nations? After all, he was the former president of a country that has been branded a rogue nation in an 'axis of evil' by the very country that granted him a travel visa. At the time, the United States and Iran were, at least rhetorically, at war. Khatami's presidency made for the conception of a persona that years later would be accepted by all, and even by American neo-conservatives. His vision and presidential style, and his frank approach to both domestic and international challenges, forged a leader out of a cleric who would be respected both at home and abroad.

In fact, Khatami's post-presidency years have been notable. While rarely making comments on day-to-day politics, he has delivered numerous lectures and keynote addresses at prestigious institutions and universities. In November 2006, he completed a world-wide lecture circuit, from Harvard University in Boston to the University of St Andrews in Scotland, where he inaugurated the Institute of Iranian Studies, and then on to the prestigious British think-tank Chatham House. The former president was nominated by Kofi Annan in 2005 to serve as a member of a United Nations-sponsored high-level task force made up of about 20 eminent personalities. The group has deliberated in different international locations with the aim of fostering respect and dialogue between Islamic and western societies.[18] Known as the *Alliance of Civilisations*, the group is co-sponsored by Spanish Prime Minister, Jose Luis Rodriguez Zapatero, and the Prime Minister of Turkey, Recep Tayyip Erdogan; however, it is commonly understood that it was born directly out of the concept of the *Dialogue Among Civilisations*. Similar to the discourse of the *Dialogue*, the *Alliance of Civilisations* is framed as a potential answer for those troubled by Samuel Huntington's 'clash of civilisations' thesis. Zapatero first suggested the idea for the alliance in a speech before the United Nations General Assembly in September 2004, about six months after the bomb attacks in Madrid that killed more than 190 people. Turkey, where more than 60 people were killed in the November 2003 suicide bombings in Istanbul, later became a co-sponsor of the project, which was eventually backed by the United Nations and more than 20 countries.

On the home front, Khatami's Tehran-based Centre for the Dialogue Among Civilisations remained active until 30 December 2007 (when President Ahmadinejad proposed to integrate the centre into a new National Centre for Research on Globalisation).[19] Founded in February 1999 after the United Nations declared 2001 the 'Year of Dialogue Among Civilizations', the centre focused on building a bridge between different cultures and promoting global interaction and dialogue. On 29 January 2006, Khatami inaugurated the Foundation for Freedom, Growth and Development of Iran (BARAN). Based in Tehran, this foundation had a social and cultural agenda promoting progress, sustainable development, freedom and dialogue with the west. Baran (literally, 'rain' in Persian) is made up of about 40 founders, with Khatami as the head of the foundation's High Council. At the first monthly gathering of Baran, Khatami continued to speak about the importance of focusing on Iranian progress and development while maintaining détente with the international community. He said:

> Holding this view point that we have a duty to liberate the world only results in a situation wherein Iran too would be lost. During the reform movement the question was: Are we responsible for liberating the whole world? At the time we

> were taking preliminary steps to help liberate the whole world. Rather our responsibility is to facilitate the development of Iran. If we carry out this task in compliance with our religious and humanitarian values, then we will have also affected the Islamic world and the world in general.

What is noteworthy is that the former president also reaffirmed his reformist policies, including the advancement of the principles of freedom and justice; the consolidation of civil society and the rule of law; and economic development and internationalisation. In his address he resumed his campaign for the rule of law with the following justification: 'The harm done by lawlessness is much more than the harm done by establishing bad laws. When there is lawlessness, chaos follows. But when bad laws are introduced and implemented, parts of national interests are ensured and other parts are wasted. It is a must for our society to move toward lawfulness'.[20]

Strengths and Weaknesses of the Reform Movement

No sooner had Khatami left the presidency than Iranian pundits and scholars began to interpret and analyse what he accomplished in his project of *eslahat.* These assessments have tended to be reserved or negative. The reform was said to be 'dead' and various autopsies of the Second of Khordad Movement were conducted by disgruntled reformists and the conservative opposition. Western observers, too, were quick to point to the failure of the movement, measuring its success with the biased yardstick of Iran's support for Hizbullah or the continued veiling of women. The preceding study has shown that reform in Iran and the development of a theocratic modernity was a far more complex and nuanced process. This complexity has made it difficult to decipher change in the tangled web of Iranian institutions and practices, and the events that occurred between 1997 and 2005. A fresh assessment is required to provide a balanced assessment of the epic challenge of democratic consolidation in a theocratic state. Here, both the strengths and the weaknesses of Khatami's social project are considered.

Critics argue that Khatami failed to achieve concrete, tangible reforms in the course of his presidency. Indeed, there were huge discrepancies between Khatami's campaign promises, popular expectation and what was really achieved. This was a methodological shortcoming: Khatami had no clear-cut notion of how political transformation from a theocracy to a vibrant and open religious democracy would come about. In fact, Khatami's notion of a 'religious democracy' was riddled with inconsistencies and, in practical terms, proved unachievable. However, as a model for change, Khatami's reform agenda represents, at least theoretically, a viable trajectory to Islamic-Iranian modernity. This had to do with duality of the proposed paradigm for change: the concept raised the ire of the conservatives, but at the same time it had the tacit approval of the Supreme Leader; it embraced the democratic aspirations of the majority, but it respected the ideals of the 1979 revolution and the *Shi'i* state as a political model, including all of its theological and moral trappings.

Another frequent criticism of Khatami was his perceived failure to exercise the political will and leadership role expected of him. Critics point to Khatami's passiveness during the student riots and claim he was not assertive enough in supporting the students' cause. As stressed above, this was far more a reflection of the constitutional limitations of the presidency and the conservative opposition than any kind of authentic measure of Khatami's objectives. We have sifted through evidence showing there was a clear disjuncture between what Khatami wanted to achieve and what he was actually capable of doing. The cardinal fact is that Khatami's movement was not a revolution, but rather the gradual social and political evolution of a post-revolutionary state and society. In fact, it can be argued that Khatami ushered in a new phase in the history of post-revolutionary Iran by inaugurating the final phase in the Iranian revolutionary cycle: the stage paradoxically characterised by the repudiation of a revolutionary style of politics.

There is no doubt that Khatami overlooked the importance of defining and describing precisely what a modernised Islamic Republic would look like. How would an Islamic democracy differ from a secular western democracy? Would Iranian civil society mean the same thing as it did in the west? What precisely was being reformed, and to what extent would the status quo change if the reform project fully materialised? Inattention to these salient questions fuelled the conservative resistance, which, in the end, stifled the movement. Khatami and his supporters needed to explain how their slogans and theories would translate in practical terms. This is not to detract from the fact that the fragility of the reform movement was largely attributed to the constitutional-institutional limitations of the president, his popular mandate and his allies, vis-à-vis the conservative religious establishment.

One lucid example is the fact that Khatami was never authorised to become a member of any political organisation, although he and his supporters had initially planned to establish a political party, which they intended to transform into the opposition. In effect, the direction and pace of the reform movement was very much guided from the bottom-up (civil society), *outside* of government structures and the political organism. With no coherent political organisation and inadequate institutional power, the reformist movement only very gradually emerged from within the evolving discourse of the press, students, intellectuals and journalists. The reformist camp set their communicative sights on the press because newspapers and journals could be established quickly, had a fast production time and an avid readership. The reformists took full advantage of voicing their views in the columns of the daily press, but this proved to be naïve. The press was an intrinsically unreliable channel to articulate the reformist cause, owing, once again, to its inherent vulnerability to the spasmodic control and attacks from entrenched conservatives.[21]

It is important to recognise and underscore the fact that not all the reformist misfortunes can be blamed on conservative resistance. In fact, the reformist front had serious organisational problems. As a broad and inclusive social movement, the Second of Khordad Front always lacked both the substance and the semblance of the coherence it needed for a unified approach to reform. The reform movement was comprised of diverse circles, groupings and constituencies – from traditional conservative clerics organised in the Association of Combatant Clerics and the Association of Lecturers of Qom Theological Seminaries, to progressive secularist intellectuals in the IIPF. There were clear differences among the reformist tendencies regarding the pace and scope of reform. The older, more established and traditional segment of the reformist front favoured a slower pace and a more limited domain of reform, compared with the younger and more modern segment. This latitude of diversity helped to maintain their unity against the conservatives, but was *ipso facto* an inherent obstacle to an integrated strategy for development.

A clear example of this would be the 2002 municipal elections when the constitutive parties of the reformist front were unable to reach an agreement on a common list of candidates in large cities. Another was the reformist disorganisation that occurred in the May 2003 election to the *Khane-ye Ahzab-e Iran* (the House of Parties). Although 70 per cent of the House of Parties was reform-orientated, they failed to consolidate their power base and curb conflict among themselves. As a result, the conservatives wrested control of the governing board, and two prominent conservative figures, Hassan Ghafuri-fard and Assadollah Badamchian, became the heads of the House of Parties.[22]

One major handicap of the reform movement was the fact that the people who voted for Khatami did so primarily as a vote of no-confidence in the ruling establishment. This negative component in its support base was a serious weakness. From an objective viewpoint, it is obvious that the movement, in effect, relied on the support of 20 million *non-partisan* voters – an electorate that was mainly united in its rejection of the opposing side. It is more than self-evident that success in making decisions to guarantee the unity and coherence of this front was extremely improbable. Abbas Abdi explains that to prevent disunity there was no alternative but to avoid tackling controversial issues. He argues that this outlook was reflected in Khatami's choice of cabinet members and executive assistants to such a degree that the economic authorities of his administration were individuals holding opposing economic perspectives.[23]

The reform movement was beset with misfortune, but it did achieve some success. While Marx maintained that revolution was the only method of basic social transformation, Khatami believed that substantive change could be achieved by peaceful social action and 'modernisation from below'. In fact, the case can be made that Khatami introduced a very different conceptualisation of social change, alongside the various types of social revolutions and anti-revolutions.[24] Khatami's project of 'modernisation from below' was a new and exciting conceptual path to an Islamic modernity. Earlier chapters have already advanced the basic idea and reviewed considerable evidence showing that the movement for Islamic reform found its roots in the forces 'from below', that is, in the demands of the public as expressed in the ballot box, through the press, in activism in NGOs and in grass-roots organisations. In addition to activity in these channels, public sentiments were expressed in a number of other ways: overcrowded lecture halls featuring the conservatives' critics, the length of the columns set aside in the popular press for 'the readers' grievances', the frequency of (illegal) labour strikes and the popularity of peaceful demonstrations for political reform.[25]

Khatami can be merited for fostering a sense of citizenry, and for creating a public that was increasingly politically mature. In the words of Faridzadeh, under Khatami 'there was a public and therefore a republic'.[26] People became more active and they developed the hope that they could define the ideals and direction of the country. Thus, by empowering the electorate, Khatami strengthened the republicanism of the regime – this was substantive reform.

Khatami's Iran witnessed the early phase of a nascent democratic movement. The future of the reformist currents in Iran relies on acknowledging the gains achieved during Khatami's presidency. As Murden explains, the development of a political model is an incremental process and cannot be achieved overnight. He makes this argument with reference to the evolution of liberalism in the west:

> Liberalism was never applied in an ideal form. Liberal ideas established influential tendencies in the politics and economic systems of Europe and North America, but they always ran alongside other forms of belief and practice. Liberalism was varyingly meshed with Christianity, kingship, class, status, nation, and the state ... People could aspire to liberal ideals while retaining elements of their pre-existing beliefs. Meshing liberalism with ideologies sometimes caused tensions within

> and between societies, but westerners lived with those contradictions over long periods.[27]

Fred Halliday advances a similar argument when he proposes that:

> Fukuyama, like many in the west, overestimated how many states had attained democracy ... First, the economic history of few, if any societies in the world had even approximated to the free market model of liberal theory – the development of Japan, Singapore, Korea, and before that of Germany and Britain relied centrally on state intervention ... Secondly, democracy was not a sudden, all or nothing event ... but a gradual process, over decades and centuries: it took Britain and the USA three hundred years and three internal wars between them to move from tyranny to the kind of qualified democracy they have now. Thirdly, liberal politics is not a single act, bestowing finality on a political system. No one can be certain that a democracy is even reasonably stable unless it has been installed for at least a generation – many have appeared only to disappear.[28]

The Legacy of the Khatami Experiment

In the post-communist regimes, the question was whether emergent institutions operated in ways that contributed to the development of democratic practices. Conversely, in Iran, the question was whether embryonic democratic practices and procedures contributed to the development of more democratic-minded institutions. In the post-Khatami years, there were cases where public participation and public opinion successfully influenced the nature of political institutions. The new sense of citizenship – with which Khatami can be credited – drove people to the ballot box for the municipal and Assembly of Experts elections, both held in December 2006. The outcome of the two elections revealed a shift from conservative, hard-line tendencies towards moderation and pragmatism. Iranian reformism was alive even under the populist-conservative president, Mahmoud Ahmadinejad, by manifesting itself as an indigenous social movement that quietly fed into the political process 'from below'. What was patently clear was that Khatami's efforts to promote civil society undeniably changed the nature of political culture and civic engagement in Iran, and this was felt well after he left office.

When President Ahmadinejad took over the leadership in 2005, he felt the same pressures for reform and modernisation that Khatami had encountered during his presidency. Although economic issues became the main concern for the Iranian public when Khatami left office, aspirations for civil society remained strong. The fact was that at the end of Khatami's presidency, society had become more complex and differentiated, and this was felt by the Ahmadinejad administration. It was also evident that the upper echelons of the state no longer had a monopoly on ideology, values and norms. Political thinking was carried forward by intellectuals, writers, film directors, women activists, student leaders and NGOs, instead of solely by the state. In other words, political culture in post-Khatami's Iran was very much shaped by elements of society, rather than exclusively by the state. Arshin Adib-Moghadam refers to this force as a 'pluralistic momentum', which he argues was not limited to a single institution, political party or even a set of ideological currents.[29]

The municipal elections and the elections to the Assembly of Experts, both held on 15 December 2006, demonstrated that reformist and moderate currents thrived in the Iranian political scene even under a conservative leadership. Both races juxtaposed supporters of Ahmadinejad against members of the reformist movement. In some cases, traditional conservatives banded loosely with reformists to oppose Ahmadinejad's allies. What was clear from a host of anecdotal accounts was that the reformists had become more seasoned in articulating their views and positions, and had recognised that in order to succeed they had to use some of Ahmadinejad's populist communicative strategies. Rather than relying on abstract democratic and idealistic themes of the past, they focussed more on 'bread-and-butter' issues such as the need for better public transportation and more accountable city officials.[30]

The elections for seats in local councils were seen as a referendum on Ahmadinejad's political gains and losses during his first 18 months in office. The majority of seats went to the more moderate conservatives who opposed Ahmadinejad's hard-line approach; reformists also made significant gains. In Tehran, where Ahmadinejad had previously been mayor, his allies secured only three of the fifteen council seats, while moderate conservatives won seven, reformers took four and an independent won one. Even though voter turnout was high across Iran, Ahmadinejad and his allies won only 20 per cent of the 113,000 seats.[31] Safdar Husseini, the reformist coalition's provincial campaign coordinator, explained that of the 1,524 people who were declared winners in the elections, 605 could be considered reformers, 438 conservatives, 429 independents and only 52 on the list of Ahmadinejad's allies.[32] Overall, the elections represented a decline in hard-line representation and a partial re-emergence of Iran's moderate tendencies.

In the parallel elections to the 86-seat Assembly of Experts, Iran's two main conservative factions were matched against each other. The choice was between the traditionalist, older wing of the revolutionary generation (the mercantilist or business-friendly conservatives, led by the pragmatic, technocratic Rafsanjani), versus the younger, more populist wing of Ahmadinejad and his religious adviser, conservative ideologue, Mohammed Taghi Mesbah-Yazdi. The Ministry of Interior reported an estimated 60 per cent turnout of the 46.5 million eligible voters and later reported that more than 28 million people had voted.[33] Different parties had several candidates in common, but the candidate list announced by the Association of Combatant Clerics captured most of the seats (68 of 86 seats, while introducing 81 candidates).[34] Significantly, Rafsanjani won the most votes in Tehran. With 1,564,197 votes, Rafsanjani's tally was double the total for his main rival, Mesbah-Yazdi.[35]

Although the elections did not have a substantive overall impact, they nonetheless demonstrated that public opinion mattered. It was the lively and vigorous sense of Iranian citizenship – the legacy of Khatami's presidency – that drove people to the polls. What is more, in both elections, the trend was towards moderation and pragmatism, the pillars of reformist thinking. More importantly, the public showed that it was a major driving force, capable of substantively shaping key political institutions.

Thanks to Khatami's years in office, the political process in Iran had become de-monopolised, no longer the exclusive domain of the state. This was a new and exciting theoretical framework for understanding Iran's transition, based on the idea that public opinion can affect substantive change. As long as Iranian politics is carried forward by the democratic momentum triggered by Khatami, Iranian reformism will continue to elicit political results. Change permeated society, and this appeared to be an ongoing trend even under the conservative leadership of President Ahmadinejad. Khatami was on the mark when he said that 'reform has been entrenched in the heart of the society and that will help reform keep going'.[36]

On 15 December 2007, Iranian reformists announced a coalition of reformist and moderate parties that would run for seats in the Eighth *Majles* in the 14 March 2008 legislative elections, in an effort to launch a comeback of moderates in Iranian politics. The coalition, according to Abdollah Nasseri, spokesman for the reformist coalition, aimed to remove extremism from political discourse, improve Iran's economic problems and restore the country's international image.[37] However, many reformists were barred from even entering the race by the pre-vote vetting procedure, which they claim aimed to hand victory to the conservatives. After the vetting process for the 290-seat assembly by the conservative-controlled Guardian Council of jurists and clerics (the body responsible for vetting prospective candidates), some 4,500 candidates, representing 30 provinces, were left to run from around 7,600 who originally signed up.

While the council insisted that it acted without bias, the reformists argued that they had been sidelined deliberately to ensure conservative dominance in Iranian politics. Some even perceived the move as a message to the reformists not to contemplate a presidential comeback in 2009. Indeed, a reformist victory in the 2008 *Majles* elections could have been the next step in the reformist resurgence – perhaps leading to the presidency – if the pattern set by conservatives is a guide. As described earlier, hard-liners clawed their way out of their political oblivion of the late 1990s, first by winning the Tehran city council vote in 2002, and then recapturing the *Majles* in 2004.

Three political groups ran for seats: hard-line and traditional conservatives, the reformists, and the centrist groups. Iran's Interior Ministry estimated a 60 per cent turnout of the 44 million eligible voters, up from 51 per cent in 2004.[38] As predicted, the conservatives claimed a victory, winning 132 seats. However, not all conservatives were staunch supporters of Ahmadinejad. 'The result of the parliamentary election does not mean the government was victorious', reported Amir Ali Amiri, election coordinator for the conservative Broad Principle-ist Front. 'Our trend is principle-ist but we are critical of the government'.[39]

The reformists won 54 seats and the remaining seats went to the independents and minorities. The reformists hailed their performance as a remarkable success with around 20 per cent of seats despite the mass veto of their candidates. Again, their relative success can be attributed to their new strategy, which placed economic issues at the top of their agenda. Drawing conclusions from their past defeats, the reformists realised that the economic problems were the main issue that occupied the Iranian people's minds and that the achievements of the conservatives were made possible due to their use of economic and social slogans and their promises to improve economic conditions in Iran.

Two conclusions can be drawn from the analysis of the March *Majles* elections. The first point is that reformists appear to be a permanent feature of the Iranian political scene. The second point is that Iranian politics was undergoing a 'return to normalcy'. In the analysis of Khatami's Iran, it has been seen that for a multitude of practical purposes Khatami tried to move Iranian politics away from tumultuous times towards a regular politics. His reform movement represented the explicit project of a return to normalcy. The politics of normalcy refers to a country that is seeking to avoid diplomatic isolation, and a nation that is seeking to rid itself of revolutionary-style politics, self-reliant economic policies and rigid social mores. The emergence in Ahmadinejad's Iran of more moderate conservatives who were critical of the president's inflationary economic policies and aggressive foreign policy rhetoric, and of supporters who called on him to tone down some of his policies, was clear evidence of this trend. This shift towards more pragmatic politics mirrored Khatami's approach, characterised by an effort to base Iran's politics on the repudiation of revolutionary politics – politically, economically and socially. In Ahmadinejad's Iran, the political compass continued to display signs of this shift towards 'normal politics' where ideological radicalism was giving way to the broader interests of a twenty-first century Iran.

CONCLUSION

One of the most interesting periods in the turbulent and relatively short history of the Islamic Republic of Iran concerns the presidency of Mohammad Khatami. During his eight-year tenure, Iran's reform movement flourished and changed the lexicon and parameters of tolerated political debate in Iran. Khatami was a political phenomenon and, as the figurehead of a reformist movement, he left an indelible impact on Iran's political landscape. Like all such phenomena, Khatami brooks no lukewarm opinions; people are almost invariably for or against him. To most Iranian reformist intellectuals, he will remain the symbol of Islamist revival and reform. To his secular critics, Khatami is perceived as a passive and timid figure incapable of implementing meaningful change owing to the constraints of his own personality as well as flaws in his methodology. In the west, he is revered for propagating a relatively liberal discourse and for promoting rapprochement; at the same time, he has been regarded by sceptics as being cut from the same cloth as religious extremists. Let us now return to and try to summarise some of the themes analysed in this book, and explore ways to move beyond these polarising views of Khatami's political legacy.

There is significant continuity between the goals and aspirations of the leadership of previous Islamic Republic administrations and the overarching policies pursued by Khatami: both wanted to sustain the original goals of the revolution by creating a just Islamic state. However, Khatami's leadership *style* differed substantially from that of his predecessors. It is well known that revolutions are cyclical and characterised by chaos and the weakening of the state, followed by a phase of post-revolutionary stabilisation. Khatami's leadership represented such a period of stabilisation. The president-reformer and the Second of Khordad Movement renounced revolution as a method and favoured gradual reform as a means of creating a more dynamic Iran based on the principle of a religious democracy. After gaining popular legitimacy through the ballot box, Khatami wasted no time in promoting political expression, pluralism, diplomatic rapprochement and economic integration.

From this point of view, it is clear enough that a flurry of initiatives under the banner of *eslahat* paved the way from Islamic revolution to Islamic reformism. These measures included greater tolerance of political expression, relaxed cultural and social mores and the first local council elections, all of which changed the way civil society related to the state. At the same time, Iran's international image was improved through active diplomatic engagement. In truth, Iran had been commonly perceived as an intransigent fanatic exporter of its brand of Islamic revolution, but then suddenly – through the person of Khatami – became an advocate of mending fences with its neighbours and the key proponent of the *Dialogue Among Civilisations.* While no significant breakthroughs were achieved on the foreign policy front, dealings with the west became practical and goal-orientated, no longer so intensively filtered through visions of geopolitical and ideological competition or the chatter of the 'clash of civilisations'. In this investigation, we have explained that the *Dialogue* was not a perfectly formed thesis. It was a noble worldwide cause but it failed to resolve Iran's issues with the international community, and in particular the United States, or with its regional Arab rivals. However, Khatami's confidence-building measures on the international front definitely helped to soften Iran's image within the global political economy. In 1997, Khatami inherited a politically stagnant society, which he gradually imbued with a greater sense of purpose. He was determined to give the Islamic Republic of Iran a new sense of legitimacy by structuring it on the rule of law and by reducing the structural gulf between regime, state and society.

Khatami, a man both religious and enlightened, represented the nature of the changes he sought to implement in Iran. A theorist in his own right, Khatami's philosophical knowledge allowed him to formulate the idiom and expressions that gave his thinking a liberal cast without departing from the confines of *Shi'i* theocratic thought. Khatami parted ways with his predecessors by creatively engineering a 'third path' that aimed to transcend the sterile trajectories of the past. The great critic and prophet of modern democracy, Alexis de Tocqueville, made a prescient observation on democracy, equality and liberty: 'I would think it a great misfortune for humanity if liberty had to take the same form in every place'.[1] It appears that Khatami ascribed to the sentiment underlying this view when he set about devising an authentic and distinct attitude towards modernity for Iran. However, bereft of institutional and constitutional resources, he did not wield the power typically associated with a chief executive. This inconsistency created widespread frustration and apathy amongst those who aspired to reform. Here was a conceivable paradigm for Islamic modernity, buttressed by a popular mandate, but at the same time severely hampered by political constraints. This was the product of an uncomfortable state of tension created by the dichotomy of a religious democracy, on the one hand, and a theocratic hierocracy, on the other.

Thus, while Khatami gave the presidency his stamp of charisma, the office itself stripped him of credibility and mystique. It was actually under Khatami that the 'reformist versus conservative' paradigm became the catchphrase for characterising the ongoing political wrangling in Iran. The Iranian political mosaic is as complex and as interwoven as the design of the most intricate Persian miniatures or carpets. The closer one looks at the minute details, the more one sees that what appears on the surface as a confrontation between two camps is in fact a network of rivalries within the framework of the system. Khatami and his reformist supporters, after their two landslide victories, were faced with resistance well beyond a simple, traditional conservative legislative opposition typical of any western liberal democracy. The movement was confronted rather by the interpenetrating contradictions of the Iranian political system. Institutional constraints severely hampered the reform project, but it is equally important to recognise that there were serious methodological shortcomings in the reform programme itself. This book has explained that Khatami's political programme was flawed in its delivery. The concept of reform, while carefully articulated, was made up of a collection of buzzwords and slogans that appealed to the demographic groups Khatami's campaign was targeting. However, these catchwords were anathema to traditionalists and ultra-conservatives who feared that the infiltration of liberal, secular, 'western' ideas and institutions would jeopardise indigenous religious norms and practices, as well as the theological foundation of the state.

Still, Khatami's movement ended up staging a democratic insurgency against conservative elements through vibrant civic activism (a flourishing press, the proliferation of informal organisations and an active citizenry that made its voice heard through the ballot box). In fact, this proactive movement revealed the strong currents of civic endeavour flowing beneath the stagnant surface of Iranian life, demonstrating the vitality of the Iranian social organism. While the politics spawned under Khatami's watch lacked a consistent cumulative pattern, they were stamped by a profound commitment to democratic goals and method. Khatami's politics demonstrably repudiated influential, mythical, anthropological theories that stress the passivity and innate authoritarianism of Islamic cultures and societies.

The reform movement ushered in a critical transition in modern Iranian history. The reverberations of Khatami's reform movement continue to resonate in the realm of local politics, where popular opinion has successfully shaped the political process. What is remarkable is that despite the conservative nature of President Ahmadinejad's regime, the drive and energy for pluralism not only survives but also prevails. This is certainly the case with the election results in the city council and in the Assembly of Experts, and even the Eighth *Majles* elections signalling the emergence of moderate conservative trends. In fact, these developments reveal that broad segments of the Iranian populace and the elite are seeking to move Iranian politics away from ideological and revolutionary governance towards the 'politics of normalcy' – the cornerstone of Khatami's political philosophy.

Khatami's identification with the politics of normalcy is one of the lasting legacies of his political programme. A pragmatist cognisant of the forces of civil society, market forces and globalisation, Khatami sought to construct a model of normality that combined western-aspired reforms with something broader, taking into account Iran's unique culture, history and place in the world. He believed that by combining the universal and the particular, a country would find what is normal for itself: too far in one direction would lead to abnormality. Khatami had effectively consigned the revolutionary period of Iran's politics to history, but carried forward the original revolutionary ideals of social justice, freedom and equality. A new chapter of normality was inaugurated: this was the essence and spirit of the path of reform. The accelerating pluralistic momentum reverberating in contemporary Iran demonstrates that Iranians are capable of eliciting political results and of carrying Islamic reform forwards. Overall, this is by far Khatami's greatest achievement.

APPENDIX I

United Nations A/RES/55/23

General Assembly

Distr.: General
11 January 2001

Fifty-fifth session
Agenda item 32
00 56077

Resolution adopted by the General Assembly

[*without reference to a Main Committee (A/55/L.30 and Add.1)*]

55/23. United Nations Year of Dialogue among Civilizations

The General Assembly,

Recalling its resolutions 53/22 of 4 November 1998 and 54/113 of 10 December 1999 entitled "United Nations Year of Dialogue Among Civilizations",

Reaffirming the purposes and principles embodied in the Charter of the United Nations, which, inter alia, call for collective effort to strengthen friendly relations among nations, remove threats to peace and foster international cooperation in resolving international issues of an economic, social, cultural and humanitarian character and in promoting and encouraging universal respect for human rights and fundamental freedoms for all,

Noting that civilizations are not confined to individual nation-States, but rather encompass different cultures within the same civilization, and reaffirming that civilizational achievements constitute the collective heritage of humankind, providing a source of inspiration and progress for humanity at large,

Bearing in mind the specificities of each civilization and the United Nations Millennium Declaration of 8 September 2000,[i] which considers, inter alia, that tolerance is one of the fundamental values essential to international relations in the twenty-first century and should include the active promotion of a culture of peace and dialogue among civilizations, with human beings respecting one another, in all their diversity of belief, culture and language, neither fearing nor repressing differences within and between societies but cherishing them as a precious asset of humanity,

Noting that globalization brings greater interrelatedness among people and increased interaction among cultures and civilizations, and encouraged by the fact that the celebration of the United Nations Year of Dialogue Among Civilizations, at the beginning of the twenty-first century, will provide the opportunity to emphasize that globalization not only is an economic, financial and technological process which could offer great benefit, but also constitutes a profoundly human challenge that invites us to embrace the interdependence of humankind and its rich cultural diversity,

Recognizing the diverse civilizational achievements of humankind, crystallizing cultural pluralism and creative human diversity,

Bearing in mind the valuable contribution that dialogue among civilizations can make to an improved awareness and understanding of the common values shared by all humankind,

---

[i] United Nations, General Assembly, *Resolution 55/2.*

Stressing the need for the universal protection and promotion of all human rights and fundamental freedoms, including the right of all peoples to selfdetermination, by virtue of which they freely determine their political status and freely pursue their economic, social and cultural development,

Underlining the fact that tolerance and respect for diversity and universal promotion and protection of human rights are mutually supportive, and recognizing that tolerance and respect for diversity effectively promote and are supported by, inter alia, the empowerment of women,

Emphasizing the need to acknowledge and respect the richness of all civilizations, to seek common grounds among and within civilizations in order to address threats to global peace and common challenges to human values and achievements, taking into consideration, inter alia, cooperation, partnership and inclusion,

Welcoming the collective endeavour of the international community to enhance understanding through constructive dialogue among civilizations,

Encouraged by the positive reception of Governments, international organizations, civil society organizations and international public opinion to the proclamation of the United Nations Year of Dialogue Among Civilizations, and welcoming the initiatives undertaken by governmental and non-governmental actors to promote dialogue,

Expressing its firm determination to facilitate and promote dialogue among civilizations,

1. *Takes note with appreciation* of the report of the Secretary-General;[ii]

[ii] United Nations, General Assembly, *United Nations Year of the Dialogue among Civilizations, A/55/492/Rev.1.*

2. *Welcomes* the convening, at the level of heads of State, of a round table on dialogue among civilizations, organized by the Islamic Republic of Iran and the United Nations Educational, Scientific and Cultural Organization, held at United Nations Headquarters on 5 September 2000 and which further contributed to the promotion of dialogue among civilizations;

3. *Invites* Governments, the United Nations system, including the United Nations Educational, Scientific and Cultural Organization, and other relevant international and non-governmental organizations to continue and further intensify planning and organizing appropriate cultural, educational and social programmes to promote the concept of dialogue among civilizations, inter alia, through organizing conferences and seminars and disseminating information and scholarly material on the subject, and to inform the Secretary-General of their activities;

4. *Calls upon* Governments to encourage all members of society to take part in promoting dialogue among civilizations and provide them with an opportunity to make contributions to the United Nations Year of Dialogue Among Civilizations;

5. *Encourages* all Governments to expand their educational curricula relative to the teaching of respect for various cultures and civilizations, human rights education, the teaching of languages, the history and philosophy of various civilizations as well as the exchange of knowledge, information and scholarships among Governments and civil society in order to promote a better understanding of all cultures and civilizations;

6. *Encourages* all Member States, regional and international organizations, civil society and non-governmental organizations to continue to develop appropriate initiatives at all levels to promote dialogue in all fields with a view to fostering mutual recognition and understanding among and within civilizations;

7. *Notes with interest* the activities undertaken and proposals made by Member States, the United Nations Educational, Scientific and

Cultural Organization and international and regional organizations, including the Organization of the Islamic Conference and non-governmental organizations, for the preparation of the United Nations Year of Dialogue Among Civilizations;

8. *Decides* to devote two days of plenary meetings at the fifty-sixth session of the General Assembly, on 3 and 4 December 2001, to the consideration of the item, including consideration of any follow-up measures, and commemoration of the United Nations Year of Dialogue Among Civilizations, and encourages Member States and observers to be represented at the highest possible political level;

9. *Invites* all Governments, funding institutions, civil society organizations and the private sector to consider contributing to the Trust Fund established by the Secretary-General in 1999 to promote dialogue among civilizations;

10. *Requests* the Secretary-General to continue to provide the necessary support for strengthening the activities pertaining to dialogue among civilizations;

11. *Also requests* the Secretary-General to submit to the General Assembly at its fifty-sixth session a substantive report on the prospect of dialogue among civilizations and the activities pertaining to the United Nations Year of Dialogue Among Civilizations;

12. *Decides* to include in the provisional agenda of its fifty-sixth session the item entitled "United Nations Year of Dialogue Among Civilizations".

60th plenary meeting
13 November 2000

APPENDIX II

Round Table: 'Dialogue Among Civilizations', United Nations, New York, 5 September 2000. Address by H. E. Mr Mohammed Khatami, President of the Islamic Republic of Iran (Verbatim transcript interpreted from Persian):

The General Assembly of the United Nations has only recently endorsed the proposal of the Islamic Republic of Iran for dialogue among civilizations and cultures. Still this proposal is daily attracting increasing support from numerous academic institutions and political organisations. In order to comprehend the grounds for this encouraging reception it is imperative to take into account the prevailing situation in our world and to ponder the reasons for widespread discontent with it. It is, of course, only natural for justice-seeking and altruistic human beings to feel discontented with the status quo. The political aspects of dialogue among civilizations have already been touched upon in various settings. Today, in this esteemed gathering, allow me instead to begin with certain historical, theoretical, and, for the most part, non-political grounds for the call to a dialogue among civilizations.

One reason, which I can only briefly touch upon today, is the exceptional geographical location of Iran, a situation connecting various cultural and civilizational domains of Asia to Europe. This remarkable situation has placed Iran on a route of political hurricanes as well as pleasant breezes, of cultural exchange and also venues for international trade. One of the unintended if only natural consequences of this strategic geographical location has been the fostering of a certain cultural sense which has formed a primary attribute of the Persian soul in the course of its historical evolution. Should we try to view this primary attribute from the vantage point of social psychology and then attempt to scrutinise the constituent elements of the Persian or Iranian spirit, we would recognise a remarkable and exceptional capacity, a capacity that we could refer to as its capacity to integrate. This capacity to integrate involves reflective contemplation of the methods and achievements of various cultures and civilizations in order to augment and enrich one's cultural repertoire. The spiritual wisdom of Sohrevardi, which elegantly synthesises and integrates ancient Persian wisdom, Greek rationalism and Islamic intuitive knowledge, presents us with a brilliantly exceptional example of the Persian capacity to integrate.

We should also note that Persian thought and culture owes an immense debt to Islam as one of its primary springs of efflorescence. Islam embodies a universal wisdom. Each and every human individual, living in each and every corner of time and place, is potentially included in the purview of Islam. The Islamic emphasis on essential human equality and its disdain for such elements as birth and blood, conquered the hearts of those yearning for justice and freedom. The prominent position, on the other hand, accorded to rational thought in Islam, and the rejection of an allegedly strict separation between human thought and divine revelation, also helped Islam to overcome dualism in both latent and manifest forms. Islamic civilization is indeed one of only a few world civilizations to have become consolidated and to have taken shape around a sacred text, in this case the noble Qur'an. The essential unity of the Islamic civilization stems from the unique call that reached all Islamic peoples and nations. Its plurality derives from the diversity of responses evoked after Islam reached various nations.

What we ought to consider in earnest today is the emergence of a global culture. Global culture cannot and ought not to overlook characteristics and requirements of native local cultures with the aim of imposing itself upon them. Cultures and civilizations that have naturally evolved among various nations in the course of history are constituted from elements that have gradually adapted to collective souls and to historical and traditional characteristics. As such, these elements cohere with each other and consolidate within an appropriate network of relationships. In spite of all constitutive plurality and diversity, a unique and harmonious form can be abstracted from the collection.

In order to provide natural unity and harmony in form and content for global culture and to prevent anarchy and chaos, all concerned parties should engage in a dialogue in which they can exchange knowledge, experience and understanding in diverse areas of culture and civilization. Today it is impossible to bar ideas from freely travelling between cultures and civilizations in disparate parts of the world. However, in the absence of dialogue among thinkers, scholars, intellectuals and artists from various cultures and civilizations, the danger of cultural homelessness seems imminent. Such a state of cultural homelessness would deprive people of solace both in their own culture and in the vast open horizon of global culture.

The notion and proposal of dialogue among civilizations undoubtedly raises numerous theoretical questions. I do not mean to belittle such intellectual and academic undertakings. Rather, I want to stress that in formulating this proposal the Government of Iran has attempted to present an alternative paradigm for international relationships. This should become clearer when we take comparative notice of already existing and prevailing paradigms that underlie international relations today. It is incumbent upon us to radically examine the prevalent master paradigm and to expound the grounds for replacing it with a new one.

In order to call on the governments and peoples of the world to follow the new paradigm of dialogue among cultures and civilizations, we ought to learn from the world's past experience, especially from the tremendous human catastrophes that took place in the twentieth century. We ought to critically examine the prevalent master paradigm in international relations based on the discourse of power and the glorification of might. From an ethical perspective, the paradigm of dialogue among civilizations requires that we give up the will for power and instead appeal to the will for empathy and compassion. Without the will for empathy, compassion and understanding there would be no hope for the prevalence of order in our world.

There are two ways to realise dialogue among civilizations. First, actual instances of the interaction and interpenetration of cultures and civilizations with each other, resulting from a variety of factors, present one mode in which this dialogue takes place. This mode of interaction is clearly involuntary and optional and occurs in an unpremeditated fashion, driven primarily by vagaries of social events, geographical situation and historical contingency. Second, alternatively, dialogue among civilizations could also mean a deliberate dialogue among representative members of various civilizations such as scholars, artists and philosophers from disparate civilizational domains. In this latter sense, dialogue entails a deliberate act based upon premeditated indulgence and does not rise and fall at the mercy of historical and geographical contingency. Even though human beings inevitably inhabit a certain historical horizon, we could still aim at meta-historical discourse. Indeed, a meta-historical discussion of eternal human questions such as the ultimate meaning of life and death, or goodness and evil, ought to substantiate and enlighten any dialogue on political and social issues. Without a discussion of fundamentals, and by simply confining attention to superficial issues, dialogue would not get us far from where we currently stand. When superficial issues masquerade as real, urgent and essential, and where no agreement, or at least mutual understanding, obtains among parties to dialogue concerning what is truly fundamental, in all likelihood misunderstanding and confusion will proliferate instead of any sense of empathy and compassion.

The movement of ideas and cultural interaction and interpenetration recur in human history as naturally and persistently as the emigration of birds in nature. Translation and interpretation have always proved to be one of the prime venues for the movement of ideas. The subtlety lies in cases where the language under translation or interpretation sounds the same as the one we use today, whereas the world, or universe of discourse to which the two languages belong, has changed over time. Particular difficulty arises when one of the parties to the dialogue attempts to communicate with another by employing a basically secularist language in an essentially sacred and spiritual discourse. By secularism here I mean the general rejection of any intuitive spiritual experience and any faith in the unseen. The true essence of humanity is more inclusive than language, and this more encompassing nature of the existential essence of humanity makes it meaningful to hope for fruitful dialogue.

It now appears that the Cartesian-Faustian narrative of western civilization should give way and begin to listen to other narratives proposed by other human cultural domains. Today, the unstoppable destruction of nature stemming from the ill-founded preconceptions of recent centuries threatens human livelihood. Should there be no other philosophical, social, political and human grounds necessitating dialogue but this pitiable relationship between humans and nature, then all selflessly peace-seeking intellectuals should endeavour to promote dialogue as urgently as they can. Another goal of dialogue among cultures and civilizations is to recognise and to understand not only the cultures and civilizations of others, but also one's own. One ought to take a step away from oneself in order to get an enhanced perspective on oneself. Seeing in essence requires taking distance in perspective, and distance provides the grounds for immersion into another existential dimension.

In dialogue among cultures and civilizations, great artists should undoubtedly get due recognition together with philosophers, scholars and theologians. For artists do not see the sea, mountain and forest as mere mines and sources of energy, oil and fuel. For the artist the sea embodies the waving music of a heavenly dance, the mountain is not just a mass of dirt and boulders, and the forest is not merely an inanimate collection of timber to cut and use. A world so thoroughly controlled by political, military and economic conditions today inevitably begets the ultimate devastation of the environment and the eradication of all spiritual, artistic and intuitive havens. To alleviate this crisis we need the magical touch and spell of the enchanted artist and the inspired poet to rescue life, at least part of it, from the iron clasp of death and to make possible the continuation of life. Poets and artists engage in dialogue within and through the sacred language of spirit and morality. That language has remained safe from the poisonous winds of time.

So far as the present relationship between man and nature is concerned, we live in tragic times. The sense of solitude and monologue and the anxiety rooted within this situation embody this tragic world. Our call to dialogue aims at soothing this sense of tragedy. In addition to poetic and artistic experience, mysticism also provides us with a graceful, profound and universal language for dialogue. Mystical experience, constituted of the revelation and countenance of the sacred in the heart and soul of the mystic, opens new existential pathways on to the human spirit. A study of mystical achievements of various nations reveals to us the deepest layers of their life experience in the most universal sense. The unified mystical meaning and content across cultures and the linguistic parallelism among mystics, despite vast cultural, historical and geographical distances, is indeed perplexing. The proposal for a dialogue among civilizations builds upon the study of cultural geography of various fields of civilization. Yet the unique and irreplaceable role of governments should never be overlooked in this process.

In the absence of governmental commitment to their affirmative vote to the resolution on dialogue among civilizations, we cannot maintain high hopes for the political consequences of this proposal. Member States of the United Nations should endeavour to remove barriers from the way of dialogue among cultures and civilizations and should abide by the basic precondition of dialogue. This fundamental principle rejects any imposition and builds upon the premise that all parties to dialogue stand on essentially equal footing.

The symbolic representation of Themis, goddess of divine law and justice, has already gained virtually global acceptance as its statue appears on judiciary courts in many nations. It is now time to ask Themis to remove her blindfold. Let us ask her to set aside the lofty scale that currently weighs political and economic might as the sole measure. Instead, she should call all parties to an open discussion in various domains of thought, culture and civilization. She ought to look observantly at the evidence with open eyes and, by freeing herself from any prior obligations, she should then finally charge citizens of the world with the task of making political, economic and cultural decisions. The escalating development of information technologies will continue to penetrate deeper layers of our lives far beyond the realm of social relationships and will form common underlying interconnections between disparate cultural and geographical regions. The science of semiotics provides us with tools to excavate such common underlying links and would form the common language we need for any dialogue. We should listen in earnest to what other cultures offer, lest by relying on profound human experiences we can seek new ways for human life.

Dialogue is not easy. It is even more difficult to prepare and open up vistas upon one's inner existence to others. A belief in dialogue paves the way for vivacious hope: the hope of living in a world permeated by virtue, humility and love, and not merely by the reign of economic indices and destructive weapons. Should the spirit of dialogue prevail, humanity, culture and civilization should prevail. We should all have faith in this triumph and we should all hope that all citizens of the world will be prepared to listen to the divine call: 'So announce the good news to my servants. Those who listen to the Word, and follow the best [meaning] in it' (*The Holy Qur'an*, XXXIX:17–18).

Let us hope that enmity and oppression will end and that the clamour of love for truth, justice and human dignity will prevail. Let us hope that all human beings will sing along with Hafez of Shiraz, that divinely inspired spirit, that: 'No ineffable clamour reverberates in the grand heavenly dome more sweetly than the sound of love'.

GLOSSARY

Akhlagh: Social and public adeptness, finesse and etiquette in character and manner.

Ayatollah: Literally, the 'sign of God'; an honorific title given to the most senior *Shi'i* Muslim religious jurists.

Basij: Literally, 'mobilisation'; in the Islamic Republic, the term denotes the volunteer Islamic militia.

Bazaari: The traditional merchant classes, operating informally through extended family networks. Most cities and towns have their *bazaar*.

Bonyad: Religious foundations or charitable trusts in Iran.

Edalatkhaneh: Literally, 'house of justice'; an independent judiciary associated with the Persian Constitutional Revolution.

Ershad: Refers to the Ministry of Islamic Culture and Guidance in Iran.

Eslahat: Literally, 'reform'.

Eslahtalabi: Derived from the term *eslahat*, the term refers to the project of reformism or support for reform.

Fatwa: An Islamic decree issued by a religious jurist on a specific issue.

Gharbzadegi: Literally, 'West-toxication'; a pejorative Persian term referring to the loss of Iranian cultural identity through the adoption and imitation of Western models and Western criteria in education, the arts and culture. Originating in the 1940s, the expression gained common usage following the clandestine publication in 1952 of Jalal Al-e Ahmad's book *Gharbzadegi*, to which he gave the subtitle *A Plague from the West*.

Gofteh-guh: Dialogue or discourse.

Hadith: The term for the recorded and collected quotations of the acts and words of Prophet Mohammad. It forms one of the foundations of Islamic jurisprudence.

Hawzeh: A term used in *Shi'i* Islam to represent Islamic academies.

Hizbullah: Literally, 'party of God'.

Hijab: Islamic attire, referring to women's head and body covering.

Ijtihad: (see *Mujtahid*).

Kadkhoda: Village headman in rural Iran; also used as the title for leaders of some tribal clans.

Khateh seh: Literally, 'third line', referring to Khatami's chosen path to reforming the Islamic Republic.

Mahdi: In Twelver *Shi'i* Islamic eschatology, the *mahdi* is the prophesied redeemer of Islam, the ultimate saviour of humankind on the 'Day of Judgement'.

Majles: Literally, 'council' or 'assembly'. In common speech, the term has come to mean 'parliament'. The Constitutional Revolution in 1906 established a 'National Consultative Assembly', and this was replaced in 1979 with the Islamic Consultative Assembly; the equivalent to a Parliament.

Mardom salari: Signifies 'popular government'.

Marja-e taqlid: Literally, 'source of emulation'; a qualification within *Shi'i* Islam acquired by only the most senior and respected Grand Ayatollahs.

Mujtahid: *Shi'i* religious scholars whose education and training in jurisprudence and Islamic legal texts allow them to practice *ijtihad*, the use of independent judgement, usually through analogical reasoning, to derive new rulings from the existing body of law.

Rahbar. Literally, 'leader'. In contemporary Iran it has come to refer to 'Supreme Leader' or the *Vali-e faqih*.

Roshankefran: Literally, 'enlightened thinkers' and usually translated as 'intellectuals'.

Sharia: The body of Islamic canon law. Among *Shi'i* Muslims, the *Sharia* includes the Qur'an and the authenticated sayings of the Prophet (*hadith*) and the Twelve Imams.

Shi'a: A member of the smaller of the two great divisions of Islam. The *Shi'a* support the claims of Imam Ali, the Prophet Mohammad's cousin and son-in-law, to be the immediate successor of the Prophet and, as the first Caliph, to be the leader of the Muslim community after the Prophet's death. On this issue the *Shi'a* divided from the *Sunnis* in the first great schism of Islam.

Sunna: The normative 'customs' of Prophet Mohammad; that is, his words, deeds and habits as remembered by Muslims and preserved in the literary form of the *hadith* reports.
The *Sunna* is second in authority only to the Qur'an.

Sunni: Refers to the larger of the two great divisions of Islam. The Sunnis, who rejected the claim of Imam Ali's line, believe that they are the true followers of the *sunna*, the guide to proper behaviour composed of the Qur'an and the *hadith*.

Taqlid: Literally, 'emulation'; refers to the acceptance of a religious ruling in matters of worship and personal affairs from a higher religious authority.

Towse-eh: Refers to the programme for economic reform and development.

Ulama: Literally, 'those with knowledge'; essentially religious scholars, used synonymously with the senior Muslim clergy.

Ummah: Literally, 'community' or 'nation'; specifically used to refer to the worldwide community of Muslims, as united by faith.

Vali-e faqih: Literally, the 'Guardian of the Jurisconsult'. The *faqih* is a *Shi'i* cleric who is an expert in religious jurisprudence, and whose mastery of the Qur'an, the traditions of Prophet Mohammad and the Twelve Imams, and the codices of *Shi'i* Islamic law permit him to render binding interpretations of religious laws and regulations.

Velayat-e faqih: Literally, the term signifies the 'Guardianship of the Jurisconsult'. The concept was elaborated by Ayatollah Khomeini to support political rule by the clergy.

NOTES

Introduction

[1] Firoozeh Kashani-Sabet, 'The evolving polemic of Iranian nationalism', in Nikkie Keddie et al (eds.), *Iran and the Surrounding World: Interactions in Culture and Cultural Politics* (University of Washington Press, 2002), p. 170.
[2] Ali M. Ansari, *Modern Iran Since 1921: The Pahlavis and After* (London, Pearson Education, 2003), p. 74.

Chapter 1

[1] British Broadcasting Corporation, *Khatami's Hometown on the Map*, http://news.bbc.co.uk/2/hi/middle_east/653919.stm
[2] Shurah-ye Baresi [Analysis Group], *Mardi az Baran: Nagofteha-ye az Zendegi-ye Seyyed Mohammad Khatami* [Man of the Rain: the Unspoken from Seyyed Mohammad Khatami's Life] (Tehran, Moassaseh Nashr va Tahghighat Zekr, 1998), p. 17.
[3] Ibid.
[4]Mohammad Khatami, *Hope and Challenge* (NY, Global Scholarly Publications, 1997), p. 1.
[5] Shurah-ye Baresi, *Mardi az Baran*, p. 18.
[6] Khatami, *Hope and Challenge*, p. 2.
[7] Mohammad Khatami, interview with author, 28 November 2005, Majorca, Spain.
[8] *NYT*, 1 February 1998.
[9] BBC, *Mohammad Reza Khatami*, http://news.bbc.co.uk/2/hi/middle_east/3052292.stm
[10] BBC, *Iran's Women Show Political Muscle*, http://news.bbc.co.uk/2/hi/middle_east/289503.stm
[11] Shurah-ye Baresi, *Mardi az Baran*, pp. 11, 13, 22.

[12] Shurah-ye Baresi, *Mardi az Baran*, pp. 18–19.
[13] Ibid.
[14] *NYT*, 1 February 1998.
[15] Mohammad Khatami, interview with author, 28 November 2005, Majorca, Spain.
[16] Ibid.
[17] This designation refers to the second highest authority on religion and law in Twelver *Shi'i* Islam, after Prophet Mohammad and the Imams.
[18] Shurah-ye Baresi, *Mardi az Baran*, p. 24.
[19] Iran Chamber Society, *Historic Personalities: Seyyed Mohammad Khatami*, http://www.iranchamber.com/history/mkhatami/mohammad_khatami.php
[20] Khatami, *Hope and Challenge*, p. 5.
[21] *NYT*, 1 February 1998.
[22] The Iranian, *Theatre Industry is as Alive as Film*, http://www.iranian.com/Arts/2000/January/Broadway/index.html
[23] Head Office of Culture and Islamic Guidance, *Introduction*, http://www.kermanershad.ir/english/Index.asp
[24] The Iranian, *Theatre Industry is as Alive as Film*, http://www.iranian.com/Arts/2000/January/Broadway/index.html
[25] *Hambastegi*, 21 Nov 2000.
[26] Khatami, *Hope and Challenge*, p. 2.
[27] Mohsen M. Milani, *The Making of Iran's Islamic Revolution* (Boulder, Westview Press, 1994), p. 201.
[28] Global Security.org, *Supreme Cultural Revolution Council*, http://www.globalsecurity.org/military/world/iran/scrc.htm

Chapter 2

[1] Mohammad Khatami, interview with author, 28 November 2005, Majorca, Spain.
[2] This expression is adapted from Richard Sakwa who discusses the concept with reference to Vladimir Putin, in *Putin: Russia's Choice* (London, Routledge, 2004).
[3] Mohammad Khatami, *Mardom Salari* [Popular Government] (Tehran, Entesharateh Tarheh Now, 1998), p. 7.
[4] State television, 19 January 1998.
[5] State television, 18 November, 1997.
[6] A. Banani, *The Modernization of Iran, 1921–1941* (Stanford UP, 1967), p. 57.

[7] Charles Issawi (ed.), *The Economic History of Iran, 1800–1914* (University of Chicago Press, 1971), p. 376.
[8] Ansari, *Modern Iran*, pp. 45–6.
[9] Ervand Abrahamian, *Iran Between Two Revolutions* (Princeton UP, 1982), pp. 138–9.
[10] George Baldwin, *Planning and Development in Iran* (Baltimore, Johns Hopkins Press, 1967), p. 10.
[11] M. Reza Ghods, *Iran in the Twentieth Century* (London, Adamantine Press, 1989), p. 111.
[12] Milani, *The Making of Iran's Islamic Revolution*, p. 34.
[13] Homa Katouzian, *The Political Economy of Modern Iran: Despotism and Pseudo-modernism 1926–1979* (NYUP, 1981), pp. 125–6.
[14] Abrahamian, *Iran Between Two Revolutions*, pp. 138–9.
[15] Shahroukh Akhavi, *Religion and Politics in Contemporary Iran* (NY, Albany, 1980), pp. 32–59.
[16] Robert Graham, *The Illusion of Power* (London, Croom Helm, 1978), p. 78.
[17] Homa Katouzian, *The Political Economy of Modern Iran: Despotism and Pseudo-modernism, 1926–1979* (New York University Press, 1981), p. 247.
[18] Katouzian, *The Political Economy of Modern Iran* (NYUP, 1981), p. 247.
[19] Roger M. Savory, 'Social development in Iran during the Pahlavi era', in George Lenczowski (ed.), *Iran Under the Pahlavis* (Stanford, Hoover Press, 1978), p. 105.
[20] Jane Carey and Andrew Carey, 'Iranian agriculture and its development, 1953–1973', *International Journal of Middle East Studies*, vol. 7, 1976, p. 303.
[21] Nameh Mazaheri, 'State repression in the Iranian bazaar, 1975–1977', *Iranian Studies*, 39:3 (September 2006).
[22] Misagh Parsa, *States, Ideologies and Social Revolutions* (Cambridge UP, 2000), pp. 212–3.
[23] Hamid R. Kusha, *The Sacred Law of Islam* (Burlington, Ashgate Publishing Company, 2002), p. 141.
[24] PBS, Wide Angle, *Handbook: Politics and Press in Iran*, http://www.pbs.org/wnet/wideangle/shows/iran/handbook3.html
[25] James A. Bill, 'Modernization and reform from above: the case of Iran', *Journal of Politics*, vol. 32, 1970, p. 29.
[26] Richard Sakwa, 'The Anti-revolutions of 1989–91', in Moira Donald (ed.), *Reinterpreting Revolution in Twentieth-century Europe* (London, Macmillan, 2001), p. 174.
[27] Reza Davari-Ardankani, *Falsafih Chist?* [What is Philosophy?], (Tehran, Anjoman-i Islami-i Hikmat va Falsafih-i Iran, 1980), pp. xxii–xxiii.

[28] Nikkie R. Keddie, *The Roots of Revolution* (Yale UP, 1981), pp. 2–3, 255–6.
[29] Mehdi Moslem, *Factional Politics in Post-Khomeini Iran* (Syracuse UP, 2002), p. 21.
[30] Hugh Barnes and Alex Bigham, *Understanding Iran: People Politics and Power* (London, Foreign Policy Centre, 2006), pp. 2–3.
[31] The power structure of the Islamic Republic is described more comprehensively in chapter 6.
[32] Said Amir Arjomand, *The Turban for the Crown* (Oxford UP, 1988), p. 165.
[33] Nadir Entessar, 'The military and politics in the Islamic Republic of Iran', in Houshang Amirahmadi and Manoucher Parvin (eds), *Post-revolutionary Iran* (London, Westview Press, 1988), pp. 64–5.
[34] Baqer Moin, *Life of the Ayatollah* (London, I.B. Tauris, 1999), p. 226.
[35] Ibid., p. 197.
[36] Moin, *Life of the Ayatollah*, p. 224.
[37] Dilip Hiro, *Islamic Fundamentalism* (London, Palladin, 1988), p. 197.
[38] Saeed Rahnema, 'Continuity and change in industrial policy', in Saeed Rahnema and Sohrab Behdad (eds), *Iran After the Revolution* (London, I.B. Tauris, 1995), p. 146.
[39] Ghoncheh Tazmini, 'Development and Revolution in Russia and Iran: Modernisation from Above, Revolutions from Below' (PhD thesis, University of Kent at Canterbury, 2004), p. 7.
[40] It must be emphasised that these were indeed 'modernities' because transformation derived from a future-orientated prescription for social organisation.
[41] Ambassador Javad Faridzadeh, interview with author, 9 September 2005, Rome, Italy.
[42] Farhad Khosrokhavar, 'The new intellectuals in Iran', *Social Compass*, 51:2 (2004), p. 198.
[43] 'West-toxication' is a term coined by Jalal Al-e Ahmad to describe the cultural disease that had plagued Iran in the 1960s. The conservatives continue to subscribe to this view.
[44] MERIP, *Do-e Khordad and the Specter of Democracy*, http://www.merip.org/mer/mer212/212_ehsani_intro.html
[45] Ambassador Javad Faridzadeh, interview with author, 9 September 2005, Rome, Italy.
[46] Najayeh Mahmoudali, 'Khatami Inghelab-e Irani-ro Nejaat Midahad' [Khatami saves the Iranian revolution], *Tarjomaan-e Siyasi* [Political Analysis], 4:12 (1999), pp. 4–5.

[47] Mohammad Khatami, *Islam, Liberty and Development* (NY, Institute of Global Cultural Studies, 1998), p. 40.
[48] Ibid., p. 52.
[49] Ibid., p. 30.
[50] Ibid.
[51] Ibid., p. 61.
[52] Ibid., p. 65.
[53] Ibid.
[54] Khatami, *Mardom Salari*, pp. 16–22.
[55] Bulent Aras, 'Transformation of the Iranian political system: towards a new model?' *Middle East Review of International Affairs*, 5:5 (September 2001), p. 4.
[56]Khatami, *Islam, Liberty and Development*, pp. 72–5.
[57] Ibid., p. 75,
[58] Ibid., pp. 75–6, 105–8.
[59] Ibid., pp. 106–7. He cites Ruhollah Khomeini, *Sahifa-yi Nur* [Pages of Light], vol. 21, p. 47.
[60] Daniel Brumberg, *Reinventing Khomeini: The Struggle for Reform in Iran* (Chicago, University of Chicago Press, 2001), pp. 135–6.

Chapter 3

[1] *Ettelaat*, 10 August 1991.
[2] Crane Brinton, *The Anatomy of Revolution* (NY, Vintage Books, 1965).
[3] Moslem, *Factional Politics*, p. 147.
[4] Patrick Clawson and Michael Rubin, *Eternal Iran* (NY, Palgrave Macmillan, 2006), p. 119.
[5] Vanderbilt University, Television News Archive, ABC Evening News, *Iraq Invasion of Kuwait/ Iran*, http://openweb.tvnews.vanderbilt.edu/1990-8/1990-08-13-ABC-8.html
[6] Robin Wright, *The Last Great Revolution: Turmoil and Transformation in Iran* (NY, Random House, 2000), p. 24.
[7] Abbas Abdi, 'The reform movement: background and vulnerability', *Global Dialogue: Iran at the Crossroads*, 3: 2–3 (Spring–Summer 2001), pp. 28–9.
[8] Ali Gheisssari and Vali Nasr, *Democracy in Iran: History and the Quest for Liberty* (Oxford UP, 2006), p. 129.
[9] Alinejad, 'Coming to terms with modernity', p. 25.
[10] Abdi, 'The reform movement', p. 30.
[11] Moslem, *Factional Politics*, pp. 69–70. He cites *Ettelaat*, 4 May 1988.

[12] Ibid., pp. 113–14.
[13] Stephen Fairbanks, 'Theocracy versus democracy: Iran considers political parties', *The Middle East Journal*, 52: 2 (1998), p. 23.
[14] *Iran*, 25 September 1996.
[15] *Iran*, 26 September 1996.
[16] *Salam*, 28 July 1996.
[17] *Resaalat*, 29 July 1996.
[18] *Iran*, 16 October 1996.
[19] Moslem, *Factional Politics*, p. 227.
[20] *Jomhuri-ye Islami*, 6 November 1996.
[21] What is interesting is that Khatami remained equally tight-lipped on whether he would run in the June 2009 presidential elections. However, he did reveal that he was concerned about being the target of a smear campaign in the media owned by his opponents during the campaign and about his ability to rectify some of the problems caused by President Ahmadinejad's administration, particularly the economy and foreign relations.
[22] Ali Gheissari and Vali Nasr, *Democracy in Iran: History and the Quest for Liberty* (Oxford UP, 2006), p. 131.
[23] Ibid.
[24] *Tehran Radio*, 5 July 1996.
[25] *Le Monde Diplomatique*, January 1998.
[26] Khatami, *Hope and Challenge*, p. 4.
[27] *Ettelaat*, 26 February 1997.
[28] *Salam*, 27 April 1997.
[29] Moslem, *Factional Politics*, p. 101. He cites *Khabar-nameh-e ye Jame'eh-e ye Rouhaniyat-e Mobarez* [Newsletter of the Society of Combatant Clerics], no. 22 (August–September 1995), p. 295.
[30] *Salam*, 17 March 1999.
[31] *Resaalat*, 15 November 1996.
[32] *Tehran Times*, 6 May 1997.
[33] *Islamic Republic News Agency, 16* May 1997.
[34] BBC, *Profile: Mohammad Khatami*, http://news.bbc.co.uk/2/hi/middle_east/1373476.stm
[35] *Islamic Republic of Iran Broadcasting*, 10 May 1997.
[36] *Jomhuri-ye Islami*, 13 May 1997.
[37] Ibid., 11 May 1997.
[38] Mohammad Reza Tajik, 'Khalbotshekafi-eh Siyasi: Ravaniyeh Yek Entekhab' [Political analysis: the psychology of an election], in Abdolali Rezai and Abbas Abdi (eds), *Entekhabateh Now: Tahlilhayeh Jaamehshenasi az*

Vagheh Dovomeh Khordad [Sociological Analysis of the Event of the Second of Khordad] (Tehran, Entesharateh Tarheh Now, 1998), pp. 87–8.
[39] *Salam*, 7 May 1997.
[40] Ibid., 18 May 1997.
[41] *Human Rights Watch/ Middle East*, New York, 21 May 1997.
[42] *Kayhan*, 21 May 1997.
[43] *Salam*, 21 April 1997.
[44] *Kar va Kargar*, 21 April 1997.
[45] *Iran News*, 7 May 1997.
[46] Election figures are from the Iranian Ministry of Interior. There are occasional discrepancies between the data reported by the Ministry of Interior, the Guardian Council and news agencies. Therefore the figures cited should be taken as approximate.
[47] Shaul Bakhash, 'Iran's remarkable election', *Journal of Democracy*, 9:1 (January 1998), p. 80.
[48] Christopher de Bellaigue, 'The struggle for Iran', *New York Review of Books*, 16 December 1999, p. 54.
[49] *Kayhan*, 23 May 1997.
[50] *Islamic Republic News Agency*, 23 May 1997.
[51] Shurah-ye Baresi, *Mardi az Baran*, p. 11.
[52] John F. Harris, 'Clinton hopeful but sceptical on new Iranian leader', *Washington Post*, 30 May 1997.
[53] Ezatollollah Fooladvand, in Massoud Razai (ed.), *Jameh-eh ye Madani, Dovomeh Khordad va Khatami* [Civil Society, the Second of Khordad and Khatami] (Tehran, Farzan, 2000), p. 24.
[54] Tajik, *Entekhabateh Now: Tahlilhayeh Jaamehshenasi az Vagheh Dovomeh Khordad*, p. 32.

Chapter 4

[1] Robert Hefner (ed.), *Remaking Muslim Politics: Pluralism, Democratization, Contestation* (Princeton UP, 2005), p. 116.
[2] *Salam*, 11 June 1997.
[3]Anoushiravan Ehteshami, 'Iran's new order: domestic developments and foreign policy outcomes', *Global Dialogue: Iran at the Crossroads*, 3:2–3 (Spring–Summer 2001), p. 48.
[4] Moslem, *Factional Politics*, p. 256.
[5] *Iranian National Broadcasting Agency*, 11 June 1997.
[6] *Reuters*, 12 August 1997.
[7] Ibid.

[8] BBC, *Iranian Moderate Escapes Impeachment*, http://news.bbc.co.uk/2/hi/middle_east/332808.stm
[9] BBC, *Profile of Abdollah Nouri*, http://news.bbc.co.uk/2/hi/middle_east/539470.stm
[10] *Ettelaat*, 5 August 1997.
[11] Khatami, *Hope and Challenge*, pp. 76–7.
[12] *Salam*, 23 October 1997.
[13] Ehteshami, 'Iran's new order', p. 47.
[14] *Iran Times* (Washington), 10 December 1999.
[15] Plan and Budget Organization, Islamic Republic of Iran, *Barnameh-ye Avval-e Tose'eh Eqtesadi, Ejtema'i, Farhangi Jomhuri-ye Islami-ye Iran, 1368–1372* [The First Economic, Social, Cultural Development Plan of the Islamic Republic of Iran, 1989–1993] 1989, pp. 27, 37.
[16] Plan and Budget Organization, Islamic Republic of Iran, *Barnameh-ye Dovvom-e Tose'eh Eqtesadi, Ejtema'i, Farhangi Jomhuri-ye Islami-ye Iran, 1373–1377* [The Second Economic, Social, Cultural Development Plan of the Islamic Republic of Iran, 1994–1998] 1993, pp. 7, 2.
[17] Centre for Women's Participation, Office of the President, *National Report on Women's Status in the Islamic Republic of Iran* (Tehran, Centre for Women's Participation, 2001), pp. 15–19.
[18] Educational Research and Planning Organization, *Amuzesh-e Herfeh va Fan* [Technical–Vocational Training] (Tehran, Ministry of Education, 2002), p. 79.
[19] United Nations Development Programme, *The First Millennium Development Goals Report, Islamic Republic of Iran*, 2004, p. 24.
[20] Parvin Paidar, 'Encounters between feminism, democracy and reformism in contemporary Iran', in Maxine Molyneux and Shahr Razavi (eds), *Gender, Justice, Development and Rights* (Oxford UP, 2002), p. 249.
[21] *Keyhan*, 12 August 1999.
[22] *Radio Free Europe/ Radio Liberty*, 3 August 2005.
[23] Ibid.
[24] *Etemaad*, 4 May 2005.
[25] *Aftab-e Yazd*, 16 June 2003.
[26] United Nations Development Programme, *Iran: Human Development Report*, 1999.
[27] Paidar in Molyneux and Razavi, 'Encounters between feminism, democracy and reformism', p. 252.
[28] MERIP, *Do-e Khordad.*
[29] United Nations Development Programme, *Non-governmental Organisations in the Islamic Republic of Iran*, p. 111.

[30] Ibid.
[31] A. William Samii, 'Dissent in Iranian elections: reasons and implications', *Middle East Journal*, 58:3 (Summer 2004), pp. 403–4. He cites Iranian Ministry of Interior statistics (http://www.moi.ir).
[32] Ministry of Culture and Islamic Guidance, *Parties in Iran*, http://www.farhang.gov.ir/iran-media/pi.htm
[33] MEMRI, *Reza Khatami: Reform is a Revolutionary Process: The Conservatives are the Enemies of Social Freedoms*, http://memri.org/bin/articles.cgi?Page=archivesandArea=sdandID=SP6 7604
[34] *Forbes Magazine*, 12 July 2003.
[35] Akbar Karbassian, 'Islamic revolution and the management of the Iranian economy', *Social Research*, 67:2 (Summer 2000), pp. 621–40.
[36] Salamiran.org, *Foreign Investment Promotion and Protection Act*, http://www.salamiran.org/Economy/investment_law.html
[37] Hefner, *Remaking Muslim Politics*, p. 130.

Chapter 5

[1] *Zeitgeist* denotes the 'spirit of the times' and reflects the cultural and intellectual climate of an era.
[2] Mohammad Khatami, 'Dialogue among civilisations and cultures', p. 72 in Akbar Ahmed and Brian Frost (eds), *After Terror: Promoting Dialogue Among Civilisations* (Cambridge, Polity, 2005). Italics are in the original.
[3] Mohammad Khatami, 'The role of religion in the dialogue among civilisations', in Achim D. Koddermann (ed.), *Dialogue Among Civilizations: A Collection of Presentations from the General Assembly of the United Nations and Invited Essays*, vol. 2 (NY, Global Scholarly Publications, 2005), pp. 17–21.
[4] Khatami in Koddermann, 'Dialogue among civilisations and cultures', p. 76.
[5] Ahmad Naghibzadeh, 'Iran and Europe: trends and prospects', *Global Dialogue: Iran at the Crossroads*, 3:2–3 (Spring–Summer 2001), p. 78.
[6]Amir M. Haji-Yousefi, 'Economic globalisation, internationalization of the state and cooperation: the case of the Islamic republic of Iran', *The Iranian Journal of International Affairs*, no. 1, Spring 2001, p. 2.
[7] Kenneth Pollack and Ray Takeyh, 'Taking on Tehran', *Foreign Affairs*, 84:2 (March–April 2005), p. 22.
[8] Gary Sick, 'The future of US–Iran relations', *Global Dialogue: Iran at the Crossroads*, 3:2–3 (Spring–Summer 2001), p. 67.
[9] *RFE/ RL*, 24 February 1998.

[10] 'Didareh Khatami va Pap va Gofteh-e Guh-e Tamaddonha' [Meeting between Khatami and the Pope and the Dialogue Among Civilisations], *Hafte-nameh Egtesaad, Eshtemahi, Farhangi*, no. 47, 12 March 1999, p. 5.
[11] Iran Chamber of Commerce, Industries and Mines Online, *Economic Outcomes of President Khatami's Visit to Italy*, http://iccim.org/english/Magazine/iran_commerce/no2_1999/08.htm
[12] *Payvand Iran News*, 29 October 2002.
[13] *RFE/ RL*, 11 February 2004.
[14] Gulfnews.com, *Iran and Saudi Leaders in Key Talks*, http://archive.gulfnews.com/articles/07/03/04/10108680.html
[15] Svante E. Cornell, 'Iran and the Caucasus: the triumph of pragmatism over ideology', *Global Dialogue: Iran at the Crossroads*, 3:2–3 (Spring–Summer 2001), p. 91.
[16] Ibid., p. 3.
[17] Jahangir Amuzegar, 'Iran's virtual democracy at a turning point', *SAIS Review*, 20: 2 (Summer–Fall) 2000, p. 99.
[18] Vladimir Orlov and Alexander Vinnikov, 'The great guessing game: Russia and the Iranian nuclear issue', *The Washington Quarterly*, 28:2 (Spring 2005), p. 54.
[19] Ariel Cohen and James Phillips, 'Countering Russian–Iranian military cooperation', *Heritage Organization, Russia and Eurasia, Backgrounder 1425*, 5 April 2001.
[20] Orlov and Vinnikov, 'The great guessing game', p. 56.
[21] Jahangir Amuzegar, 'Khatami's first term presidency: an outsider's assessment', *SAIS Review*, 22:1 (Winter–Spring 2002), p. 7.
[22] IAEA.org, *Iran Signs Additional Protocol on Nuclear Safeguards*, http://www.iaea.org/NewsCenter/News/2003/iranap20031218.html
[23] *International Herald Tribune*, 12 August 2005.
[24] CNN, *The Iran Brief 6/2*, 27 May 1997.
[25] Hossein Alikhani, *Sanctioning Iran: Anatomy of a Failed Policy* (London, I.B. Tauris, 2000), pp. 320–33.
[26] Madeleine K. Albright, *Remarks at 1998 Asia Society Dinner*, 17 June 1998, as released by the Office of the Spokesman, US Department of State, 18 June 1998.
[27] This information appears in a study conducted by the Strategic Studies Institute (United States Army War College), *Getting Ready for a Nuclear-ready Iran*, http://www.strategicstudiesinstitute.army.mil/pdffiles/pub629.pdf
[28] Sick, 'The future of Iran–US relations', p. 68.

[29] Jahangir Amuzegar, 'Iran's crumbling revolution', *Foreign Affairs*, 82:1 (January–February 2003), pp. 44–5.
[30] David Menashri, 'Implications of America's dual-trac approach to Iran', *Tel Aviv Notes*, no. 47, 22 August 2002.
[31] The White House, *The President Delivers State of the Union Address*, http://www.whitehouse.gov/news/releases/2002/01/20020129-11.html
[32] Pollack and Takeyh, 'Taking on Tehran', pp. 20-34.
[33] Angelfire, *Khatami Praises Hizbullah Fight Against Israel in Lebanon*, http://www.angelfire.com/il/FourMothers/Khatami.html
[34] Pirouz Mojtahed Zahed, 'Geopolitics and reform under Khatami', *Global Dialogue: Iran at the Crossroads*, 3:2–3 (Spring–Summer 2001), p. 58.

Chapter 6

[1] Ira Lapidus, 'Review of Elaine Sciolino's *Persian Mirrors: The Elusive Face of Iran*', *The New York Times*, 25 September 2000.
[2] Moslem, *Factional Politics*, p. 37.
[3] Eric Rouleau, 'Theocracy or democracy', *Global Dialogue: Iran at the Crossroads*, 3:2–3 (Spring–Summer 2001), p. 4.
[4] Puneet Talwar, 'Iran in the balance', *Foreign Affairs*, 80:4 (July–August 2001), p. 64.
[5] *Azad*, 30 September 1997.
[6] *Resaalat*, 25 November 1997.
[7] *Resaalat*, 20 November 1997.
[8] Ibid., 2 November 1997.
[9] *Shoma*, 10 April 1997.
[10] *Mobin*, 21 December 1998.
[11] *Resaalat*, 24 July 1998.
[12] *Iran*, 20 November 1997.
[13] Text of Gholamhossein Karbaschi's Trial, (Tehran, Farhang va Andisheh, 1998).
[14] In November 1997, Montazeri infuriated conservatives by calling for a sharp reduction in the Supreme Leader's powers.
[15] Moslem, *Factional Politics*, p. 261. Italics in the original.
[16] *Keyhan*, 15 November 1997.
[17] Ibid.
[18] *Bahay-e Azadi*, text of Mohsen Kadivar's trial (Tehran, Nashreh Ney, 2000).
[19] *Human Rights Watch*, 28 July 1999.

[20] *Sobh-e Imruz*, 5 January 1999.
[21] Abdolkarim Soroush, *Challenging the Government of God: The Iranian Reform and its Permutations*,
http://www.drsoroush.com/English/On_DrSoroush/E-CMO-20021214-Ahmad_Sadri.html
[22]*The Wall Street Journal*, 23 September 1999.
[23] *Iran Daily*, 11 July 1999.
[24] *Hamshahri*, 10 July 1999.
[25] *IRNA*, 9 July 2001.
[26] *IRNA*, 18 July 2001.
[27] *IRNA*, 2 August 2001.
[28] *Reuters*, 19 November 1999.
[29] Amuzegar, 'Iran's virtual democracy', p. 97.
[30] *Tehran Times*, 25 April 2000.
[31] *Voice of the Islamic Republic*, Radio 1, Tehran, 6 August 2000.
[32] MERIA, *Sisyphus' Newsstand: The Iranian Press Under Khatami*,
http://meria.idc.ac.il/journal/2001/issue3/samii.pdf
[33] *Aftab-e Yazd*, 8 August 2001.
[34] *IRNA*, 20 August 2001.
[35] *Aftab-e Yazd*, 12 June 2003.
[36] *IRNA*, 15 June 2003.
[37] *Aftab-e Yazd*, 19 June 2003.
[38] *IRNA*, 23 June 2003.
[39] BBC, *Khatami Keeps Iran Guessing*,
http://news.bbc.co.uk/2/hi/middle_east/1303494.stm
[40] Iran Press Service, *Khatami Enters Presidential Race*,
http://www.iran-press-service.com/articles_2001/may_2001/khatami_candidacy_update_4501.htm
[41] Christopher de Bellaigue, 'Iran's last chance for reform?', *Washington Quarterly*, 24:4 (Autumn 2001), p. 71.
[42] Ibid.
[43] *IRNA*, 18 July 2001.
[44] *Iran News*, 8 August 2001; *IRNA*, 6 August 2001.
[45] *IRNA*, 7 August 2001.
[46] *Iran News*, 6 August 2001.
[47] *NYT*, 9 August 2001.
[48] *Iran News*, 13 August 2001; *Tehran Times*, 13 August 2001.
[49] 'The reform nobody wants anymore: Iran's elections, *ISIM Review*, no. 15, Spring 2005, p. 42.

[50] Samii, 'Dissent in Iranian elections', pp. 418, 404. He cites the Iranian Ministry of Interior figures.
[51] Reza Davari-Ardakani, *Enqeleab-e Eslami va Vaz-e Konuni-ye Alam* [Islamic Revolution and the Present Status of the World] (Tehran, Entesharat-e Markaz-e Farhangi-ye Allameh Tabatabai, 1983), p. 83.
[52] Seyyed Asadollah Athary Maryan, 'Challenge between tradition and modernity in Iran', *Discourse: an Iranian Quarterly*, 2:2 (Fall 2000), p. 68.
[53] Dr. Reza Davari-Ardakani, interview with author, 11 August 2005, Academy of Islamic Sciences, Tehran, Iran.
[54] 'Goftoguy-e Adyan va Tafahom-e Howzahha-ye Farhangi' [Inter-religious dialogue and mutual understanding in cultural fields] *Nameh Farhang*, 2:4 (1992), p. 10.
[55] Vala Vakili, 'Political opinion of Abdolkarim Sorush: dialogue between religion and politics in Iran', Said Mohebi (tr.), *Kiyan*, 7:37 (May–June 1997), p. 27.
[56] A. Matin-Asghari, 'Abdolkarim Soroush and the secularization of Islamic thought in Iran', *Iranian Studies*, 30:1–2 (1997), p. 104.
[57] Abdolkarim Sorush, *Siratha-ye Mustaqim* [Straight Paths] (Tehran, Sirat, 1998), pp. 1, 49.
[58] Dariush Ashuri, 'Guft Manha-yi Rawshanfikri: Gharbzadegi, Rawshanfekri-ye dini', *Rah-i Naw*, 1:9 (1998), pp. 20–1.
[59] *The Wall Street Journal*, 8 December 2004.
[60] Kamran Giti, 'Opponents of reform: tradition in the service of radicalism', *Global Dialogue: Iran at the Crossroads*, 3:2–3 (Spring–Summer 2001), p. 42.
[61] MERIP, *Do-e Khordad.*
[62] *IRNA*, 1 September 2004.
[63] *Financial Times*, 25 September 2004.

Chapter 7

[1] Simon W. Murden, *Islam, the Middle East and the New Global Hegemony* (London, Lynne Reinner Publishers, 2002), p. 1.
[2] Fred Halliday, *The Middle East in International Relations: Power, Politics and Ideology* (Cambridge UP, 2005). He cites Abdessalam Yassine, *Islamiser la modernité*, Al Ofok Impressions, 1998, p. 254.
[3] Ruhollah Khomeini, *Sahifa-yi Imam* [Pages of the Imam] (Tehran, Ministry of Culture and Islamic Orientation Press, 1999), vol. 9, p. 18.
[4] Sussan Siavoshi, 'Ayatollah Khomeini and the contemporary debate on freedom', *Journal of Islamic Studies*, 18:1 (2007).

[5] Ervand Abrahamian, *Khomeinism* (Berkeley, UCLA, 1993), p. 2.
[6] Siavoshi, 'Ayatollah Khomeini and the contemporary debate on freedom', p. 27.
[7] Ibid., p. 38.
[8] Ruhollah Khomeini, *Sahifa-yi Nur* [Pages of Light] (Tehran, Ministry of Culture and Islamic Orientation Press, 2000), vol. 5, p. 122.
[9] Ibid., vol. 14, p. 73.
[10] RFE/RL, *Judiciary: Iran Orders Ban on Torture*, http://www.rferl.org/featuresarticle/2004/04/0b1aad92-26b0-4696-8220-fdd31801f1e0.html
[11] Khomeini, *Sahifa-yi Imam*, vol. 5, p. 409.
[12] Khomeini, *Sahifa-yi Nur*, vol. 9, p. 186.
[13] *The Independent*, 18 December 2006.
[14] BBC, *Profile: Mohammad Khatami.*
[15] Ambassador Mohammad Javad Faridzadeh, interview with author, 9 September 2005, Rome, Italy.
[16] Alternet, *Signs of Life in Iran's Reform Movement*, http://www.alternet.org/audits/31513/
[17] *NYT*, 30 August 2006.
[18] BBC, *Spain Proposes Cultural Alliance*, http://news.bbc.co.uk/2/hi/europe/3679336.stm
[19] AFP, 30 December 2007.
[20] *Iran Daily*, 19 March 2006.
[21] Ibid., p. 34. He cites official statistics from the Iran's Ministry of Interior.
[22] Shargh Newspaper Online, *Tahlil az Saazmandehi Tashkilateh Do Jena*, http://www.sharghnewspaper.com/821010/polit.htm
[23] Abdi, 'The reform movement', p. 33.
[24] Sakwa in Donald, 'The Anti-revolutions of 1989–91'.
[25] Amuzegar, 'Iran's virtual democracy', p. 97.
[26] Moslem, *Factional Politics*, p. 253.
[27] Murden, *Islam, the Middle East and the New Global Hegemony*, pp. 1–2.
[28] Halliday, The Middle East in International Relations, p. 159.
[29] Arshin Adib-Moghadam, 'The pluralistic momentum in Iran and the future of the reform movement', *Third World Quarterly*, 27:4 (May 2006), p. 672.
[30] Boston.com, *Iran Vote Seen as Referendum on Ahmadinejad*, http://www.boston.com/news/world/middleeast/articles/2006/12/15/iran_vote_seen_as_referendum_on_ahmadinejad/

[31] Ed Blanche, 'The shark, the crocodile and the silent coup', *The Middle East*, February 2007, issue 375, p. 20.
[32] *RFE/ RL*, 19 December 2006.
[33] IRNA, *Poshtibani-eh Bahshookoo-ye Mardom az Velayat-eh Faqih Ast* [Abundant Support of the People Emanates from the Supreme Leader], http://www.irna.ir/fa/news/view/line-5/8509309618114858.htm
[34] Baztab, *Arayesh Pirooz dar Entekhabateh-e Khobregan* [Victorious Strategy in the Election of the Assembly of Experts], http://www.baztab.com/news/55753.php
[35] Iranian Student's News Agency, *Nataayejeh Ghati Entekhabateh Khobregan-e Rahbari dar Ostaneh Tehran Elam Shod* [Final Results for the Assembly of Experts Election in the Province of Tehran], http://www.isna.ir/Main/NewsView.aspx?ID=News-846591andLang=P
[36] Alternet, *Signs of Life in Iran's Reform Movement*, http://www.alternet.org/audits/31513/
[37] Associated Foreign Press, 5 January 2008.
[38] AP, 16 March, 2008.
[39] AFP, 17 March, 2008.

Conclusion

[1] Hugh Brogan, *Alexis de Tocqueville: A Life* (Yale UP, 2007).

REFERENCES

Abrahamian, Ervand, *Iran Between Two Revolutions* (Princeton University Press, 1982).

Abrahamian, Ervand, *Khomeinism* (Berkeley, UCLA, 1993).

Ahmed, Akbar and Brian Frost (eds), *After Terror: Promoting Dialogue Among Civilisations* (Cambridge, Polity, 2005).

Akhavi, Shahroukh, *Religion and Politics in Contemporary Iran* (NY, Albany, 1980).

Amirahmadi, Houshang and Manoucher Parvin (eds), *Post-revolutionary Iran* (London, Westview Press, 1988).

Alikhani, Hossein, *Sanctioning Iran: Anatomy of a Failed Policy* (London, I.B. Tauris, 2000).

Ansari, Ali M., *Modern Iran Since 1921: The Pahlavis and After* (London, Pearson Education, 2003).

Arjomand, Said Amir, *The Turban for the Crown* (Oxford University Press, 1988).

Bakhash, Shaul, *The Reign of the Ayatollahs* (London, I.B. Tauris, 1985).

Baldwin, George, *Planning and Development in Iran* (Baltimore, Johns Hopkins Press, 1967).

Banani, A, *The Modernization of Iran, 1921–1941* (Stanford University Press, 1967).

Barnes, Hugh and Alex Bigham, *Understanding Iran: People Politics and Power* (London, Foreign Policy Centre, 2006).

Brinton, Crane, *The Anatomy of Revolution* (NY, Vintage Books, 1965).

Brogan, Hugh, *Alexis de Tocqueville: A Life* (Yale University Press, 2007).

Brumberg, Daniel, *Reinventing Khomeini: The Struggle for Reform in Iran* (Chicago, University of Chicago Press, 2001).

Clawson, Patrick and Michael Rubin, *Eternal Iran* (NY, Palgrave Macmillan, 2006).

Donald, Moira (ed.), *Reinterpreting Revolution in Twentieth-century Europe* (London, Macmillan, 2001).

Enayat, Hamid, *Modern Islamic Political Thought* (London, I.B. Tauris, 2005).

Gieling, S. *Religion and War in Revolutionary Iran* (London, I.B. Tauris, 1999).

Ghani, Cyrus, *Iran and the Rise of Reza Shah: From Qajar Collapse to Pahlavi Rule* (London, I.B. Tauris, 2001).

Gheissari, Ali and Vali Nasr, *Democracy in Iran: History and the Quest for Liberty* (Oxford University Press, 2006).

Ghods, M. Reza, *Iran in the Twentieth Century* (London, Adamantine Press, 1989).

Graham, Robert, *The Illusion of Power* (London, Croom Helm, 1978).

Halliday, Fred, *The Middle East in International Relations: Power, Politics and Ideology* (Cambridge University Press, 2005).

Hefner, Robert (ed.), *Remaking Muslim Politics: Pluralism, Democratization, Contestation* (Princeton University Press, 2005).

Hiro, Dilip, *Islamic Fundamentalism* (London, Palladin, 1988).

Issawi, Charles (ed.), *The Economic Development of Iran, 1800–1914* (University of Chicago Press, 1971).

Katouzian, Homa, *State and Society in Iran: The Eclipse of the Qajars and the Emergence of the Pahlavis* (I.B. Tauris, 2000).

Katouzian, Homa, *The Political Economy of Modern Iran: Despotism and Pseudo-modernism, 1926–1979* (New York University Press, 1981).

Keddie, Nikkie R. et al (eds), *Iran and the Surrounding World: Interactions in Culture and Cultural Politics* (Washington, University of Washington Press, 2002).

Keddie, Nikkie R., *The Roots of Revolution: An Interpretive History of Iran* (Yale University Press, 1981).

Khatami, Mohammad, *Islam, Liberty and Development* (NY, Institute of Global Cultural Studies, 1998).

Khatami, Mohammad, *Hope and Challenge* (NY, Global Scholarly Publications, 1997).

Koddermann, Achim D. (ed.), *Dialogue Among Civilizations: A Collection of Presentations from the General Assembly of the United Nations and Invited Essays*, vol. 2 (NY, Global Scholarly Publications, 2005).

Kusha, Hamid R., *The Sacred Law of Islam* (Burlington, Ashgate Publishing Company, 2002).

Lenczowski, George (ed.), *Iran Under the Pahlavis* (Stanford, Hoover Press, 1978).

Martin, Vanessa, *Creating an Islamic State: Khomeini and the Making of a New Iran* (London, I.B. Tauris, 2000).

Melzer, Arthur et al (eds), *History and the Idea of Progress* (NY, Ithaca, 1995).

Milani, Mohsen M., *The Making of Iran's Islamic Revolution* (Boulder, CO, Westview Press, 1994).

Moin, Baqer, *Khomeini: Life of the Ayatollah* (London: I.B. Tauris, 1999).

Molyneux, Maxine and Shahr Razavi (eds), *Gender, Justice, Development and Rights* (Oxford University Press, 2002).

Moslem, Mehdi, *Factional Politics in Post-Khomeini Iran* (Syracuse University Press, 2002).

Murden, Simon W., *Islam, the Middle East and the New Global Hegemony* (London, Lynne Reinner Publishers, 2002).

Parsa, Misagh, *States, Ideologies and Social Revolutions* (Cambridge University Press, 2000).

Rahnema, Saeed and Sohrab Behdad (eds), *Iran After the Revolution* (London, I.B. Tauris, 1995).

Sakwa, Richard, *Putin: Russia's Choice* (London, Routledge, 2004).

Tazmini, Ghoncheh, 'Parallel Histories of Development and Revolution in Russia and Iran: Modernisation from Above, Revolution from Below' (PhD thesis, University of Kent at Canterbury, 2004).

Wright, Robin, *The Last Great Revolution: Turmoil and Transformation in Iran* (NY, Random House, 2000).

Zubaida, S., Islam: *The People and the State: Political Ideas and Movements in the Middle East* (London, I.B. Tauris, 1993).

Journal Articles

Abdi, Abbas, 'The reform movement: background and vulnerability', *Global Dialogue: Iran at the Crossroads*, 3:2–3 (Spring–Summer 2001).

Adib-Moghadam, Arshin, 'The pluralistic momentum in Iran and the future of the reform movement', *Third World Quarterly*, 27:4 (May 2006).

Alinejad, Mahmoud, 'Coming to terms with modernity: Iranian intellectuals and the emerging public sphere', *Islam and Christian–Muslim Relations*, 13:1 (2002).

Amuzegar, Jahangir, 'Iran's crumbling revolution', *Foreign Affairs*, 83:1 (January–February 2003).

Amuzegar, Jahangir, 'Iran's virtual democracy at a turning point', *SAIS Review*, 20:2 (Summer–Fall 2000).

Amuzegar, Jahangir, 'Khatami's first term presidency: an outsider's assessment', *SAIS Review*, 22:1 (Winter–Spring 2002).

Aras, Bulent, 'Transformation of the Iranian political system: towards a new model?' *Middle East Review of International Affairs*, 5:5 (September 2001).

Bakhash, Shaul, 'Iran's remarkable election', *Journal of Democracy*, 9:1 (January 1998).

Bill, James A., 'Modernization and reform from above: the case of Iran', *Journal of Politics*, 32:1 (February 1970).

Carey, Jane and Andrew Carey, 'Iranian agriculture and its development: 1953–1973', *International Journal of Middle East Studies*, vol. 7, 1976.

Cornell, Svante E., 'Iran and the Caucasus: the triumph of pragmatism over ideology', *Global Dialogue: Iran at the Crossroads*, 3:2–3 (Spring–Summer 2001).

De Bellaigue, Christopher, 'Iran's last chance for reform?', *Washington Quarterly*, 24:4 (Autumn 2001).

Ehteshami, Anoushirvan, 'Iran's new order: domestic developments and foreign policy outcomes', *Global Dialogue: Iran at the Crossroads*, 3:2–3 (Spring–Summer 2001).

Fairbanks, Stephen, 'Theocracy versus democracy: Iran considers political parties', *Middle East Journal*, 52:2 (1998).

Giti, Kamran, 'Opponents of reform: tradition in the service of radicalism', *Global Dialogue: Iran at the Crossroads*, 3:2–3 (Spring–Summer 2001).

Haji-Yousefi, Amir M. 'Economic globalization, internationalization of the state and cooperation: the case of the Islamic Republic of Iran', *Iranian Journal of International Affairs*, no. 1, Spring 2001.

Huntington, Samuel, 'The clash of civilizations?' *Foreign Affairs*, vol. 72, Summer 1993.

Karbassian, Akbar, 'Islamic revolution and the management of the Iranian economy', *Social Research*, 67:2 (Summer 2000), pp. 621–40.

Khosrokhavar, Farhad, 'The new intellectuals in Iran', *Social Compass*, 51:2 (2004).

Matin-Asghari, A., 'Abdolkarim Soroush and the secularization of Islamic thought in Iran', *Iranian Studies*, 30:1–2 (1997).

Maryan, Seyyed Asadollah Athary, 'Challenge between tradition and modernity in Iran', *Discourse, Iranian Quarterly*, 2:2 (Fall 2000).

Mazaheri, Nimah, 'State repression in the Iranian bazaar, 1975–1977', *Iranian Studies*, 3:3 (September 2006).

Mojtahed Zahed, Pirouz, 'Geopolitics and reform under Khatami', *Global Dialogue: Iran at the Crossroads*, 3:2–3 (Spring–Summer 2001).

Naghibzadeh, Ahmad, 'Iran and Europe: trends and prospects', *Global Dialogue: Iran at the Crossroads*, 3:2–3 (Spring–Summer 2001).

Orlov, Vladimir A. and Alexander Vinnikov, 'The great guessing game: Russia and the Iranian nuclear issue', *Washington Quarterly*, 28:2 (Spring 2005).

Pollack, Kenneth and Ray Takeyh, 'Taking on Tehran', *Foreign Affairs*, 84:2 (March–April 2005).

Rouleau, Eric, 'Theocracy or democracy', *Global Dialogue: Iran at the Crossroads*, 3:2–3 (Spring–Summer 2001).

Samii, A. William, 'Dissent in Iranian elections: reasons and implications', *Middle East Journal*, 58:3 (Summer 2004).

Siavoshi, Sussan, 'Ayatollah Khomeini and the contemporary debate on freedom, *Journal of Islamic Studies*, 18:1 (2007).

Sick, Gary, 'The future of US–Iran relations', *Global Dialogue: Iran at the Crossroads*, 3:2–3 (Spring–Summer 2001).

Talwar, Puneet, 'Iran in the balance', *Foreign Affairs*, 80:4 (July–August 2001).

Vala Vakili, 'Political opinion of Abdolkarim Sorush: dialogue between religion and politics in Iran', Said Mohebi (tr.), *Kiyan*, 7:37 (May–June 1997).

Well, Mathew C., 'The Freud/Weber connection: The case of Islamic Iran', *Journal for the Psychoanalysis of Culture and Society*, 8:2 (Fall 2003).

Persian Books and Persian Journal Articles

Ashuri, Dariush, 'Guft manha-yi rawshanfikri: gharbzadegi, rawshanfekri-ye dini', *Rah-i Now*, 1:9 (1998).

Davari-Ardakani, Reza, *Enqelab-e Eslami va Vaz-e Konuni-ye Alam* [Islamic Revolution and the Present Status of the World] (Tehran, Entesharateh Markaz-e Farhangi-ye Allameh Tabatabai, 1983).

Davari-Ardakani, Reza, *Falsafih Chist?* [What is Philosophy?] (Tehran, Anjoman-i Islami-i Hikmat va Falsafih-i Iran, 1980).

Khatami, Mohammad, *Mardom Salari* [Popular Government] (Tehran, Entesharateh Tarheh Now, 1998).

Khomeini, Ruhollah, *Sahifa-yi Imam* [Pages of the Imam] (Tehran, Ministry of Culture and Islamic Orientation Press, 1999).

Khomeini, Ruhollah, *Sahifa-yi Nur* [Pages of Light] (Tehran, Ministry of Culture and Islamic Orientation Press, 2000).

Mahmoudali, Najayeh, 'Khatami inghelab-e Irani-ro nejaat midahad' [Khatami saves the Iranian revolution], *Tarjomaan-e Siyasi* [Political Analysis], 4:12 (1999).

Razai, Massoud (ed.), *Jameh-eh ye Madani, Dovomeh Khordad va Khatami* [Civil Society, the Second of Khordad and Khatami] (Tehran, Farzan, 2000).

Rezai, Abdolali and Abbas Abdi (eds), *Entekhabateh Now: Tahlilhayeh Jaamehshenasi az Vagheh Dovomeh Khordad* [Sociological Analysis of the Event of the Second of Khordad] (Tehran, Entesharateh Tarheh Now, 1998).

Soroush, Abdolkarim, *Siratha-ye Mustaqim* [Straight Paths] (Tehran, Sirat, 1998).

'Shurah-ye Baresi [Analysis Group], *Mardi az Baran: Nagofteha-ye az Zendegi-ye Seyyed Mohammad Khatami* [Man of the Rain: The Unspoken from Seyyed Mohammad Khatami's Life] (Tehran, Moassaseh Nashr va Tahghighat Zekr, 1998).

World Wide Web Sites (as accessed December 2008)

Alternet, *Signs of Life in Iran's Reform Movement*, http://www.alternet.org/audits/31513/

Angelfire, *Khatami Praises Hizbullah Fight against Israel in Lebanon*, http://www.angelfire.com/il/FourMothers/Khatami.html

Bank of England, *Speech by The Right Honourable Eddie George: Iran Invest 2000 Conference*, http://www.bankofengland.co.uk/publications/speeches/2000/speech100.htm

Baztab, *Arayesh Pirooz dar Entekhabateh Khobregan* [Victorious Strategy in the Election of the Assembly of Experts], http://www.baztab.com/news/55753.php

BBC, *Iran's Disappointed Women*, http://news.bbc.co.uk/2/hi/middle_east/3500565.stm

BBC, *Iranian Moderate Escapes Impeachment*, http://news.bbc.co.uk/2/hi/middle_east/332808.stm

BBC, *Iran's Women Show Political Muscle*, http://news.bbc.co.uk/2/hi/middle_east/289503.stm

BBC, *Khatami's Hometown on the Map*, http://news.bbc.co.uk/2/hi/middle_east/653919.stm

BBC, *Khatami Keeps Iran Guessing*, http://news.bbc.co.uk/2/hi/middle_east/1303494.stm

BBC, *Profile: Mohammad Khatami*, http://news.bbc.co.uk/2/hi/middle_east/1373476.stm

BBC, *Profile: Mohammad Reza Khatami*, http://news.bbc.co.uk/2/hi/middle_east/3052292.stm

BBC, *Profile of Abdollah Nouri*, http://news.bbc.co.uk/2/hi/middle_east/539470.stm

BBC, *Spain Proposes Cultural Alliance*, http://news.bbc.co.uk/2/hi/europe/3679336.stm

Boston.com, *Iran Vote Seen as Referendum on Ahmadinejad*, http://www.boston.com/news/world/middleeast/articles/2006/12/15/iran_vote_seen_as_referendum_on_ahmadinejad/

Global Security.org, *Supreme Cultural Revolution Council*, http://www.globalsecurity.org/military/world/iran/scrc.htm

Gooya, *Jepeh-ye Abshakerat* [Participation Front], http://news.gooya.com/president84/archives/031420.php

Gulfnews, Iran and Saudi Leaders in Key Talks, http://archive.gulfnews.com/articles/07/03/04/10108680.html

Head Office of Culture and Islamic Guidance, Introduction, http://www.kermanershad.ir/english/Index.asp

IAEA.org, Iran Signs Additional Protocol on Nuclear Safeguards, http://www.iaea.org/NewsCenter/News/2003/iranap20031218.html

Iran Chamber of Commerce, Industries and Mines Online, Economic Outcomes of President Khatami's Visit to Italy, http://iccim.org/english/Magazine/iran_commerce/no2_1999/08.htm

Iran Chamber Society, Historic Personalities: Seyyed Mohammad Khatami, http://www.iranchamber.com/history/mkhatami/mohammad_khatami.php

Iran Press Service, Khatami Enters Presidential Race, http://www.iran-press-service.com/articles_2001/may_2001/khatami_candidacy_update_4501.htm

IRNA, Poshtibani-eh Bahshookoo-ye Mardom az Velayat-eh Faqih Ast [Abundant Support of the People Emanates from the Supreme

Leader], http://www.irna.ir/fa/news/view/line-5/8509309618114858.htm

IRNA, People's High Turnout in Elections Boosts Iran's Prestige: Jannati, http://www.irna.ir/en/news/view/line-24/0612229130142333.htm

ISNA, Nataayejeh Ghati Entekhabateh Khobregan-e Rahbari dar Ostaneh Tehran Elam Shod [Final Results for the Assembly of Experts Election in the Province of Tehran Announced], http://www.isna.ir/Main/NewsView.aspx?ID=News-846591andLang=P

MEMRI, Reza Khatami: Reform is a Revolutionary Process: The Conservatives are the Enemies of Social Freedoms, http://memri.org/bin/articles.cgi?Page=archivesandArea=sdandID=SP67604

MEMRI, Sisyphus' Newsstand: The Iranian Press Under Khatami, http://meria.idc.ac.il/journal /2001/issue3/samii.pdf

MERIP, Do-e Khordad and the Specter of Democracy, http://www.merip.org/mer/mer212/212_ehsani_intro.html

Ministry of Culture and Islamic Guidance, Parties in Iran, http://www.farhang.gov.ir/iran-media/pi.htm

Ministry of Interior of the Islamic Republic of Iran, www.moi.ir

PBS, Wide Angle, *Handbook: Politics and Press in Iran*, http://www.pbs.org/wnet/wideangle/shows/iran/handbook3.html

RFE/RL, *Judiciary: Iran Orders Ban on Torture*, www.rferl.org/featuresarticle/2004/04/0b1aad92-26b0-4696-8220-fdd31801f1e0.html

Salamiran.org, *Foreign Investment Promotion and Protection Act*, http://www.salamiran.org/Economy/investment_law.html.

Shargh Newspaper Online, *Tahlil az Saazmandehi Tashkilateh Do Jena* [Analysis of the Organisation of Two Parties], http://www.sharghnewspaper.com/821010/polit.htm

Soroush, Abdolkarim, *Challenging the Government of God: The Iranian Reform and its Permutations*, http://www.drsoroush.com/English/On_DrSoroush/E-CMO-20021214-Ahmad_Sadri.html

Strategic Studies Institute (United States Army War College), *Getting Ready for a Nuclear-ready Iran*, http://www.strategicstudiesinstitute.army.mil/pdffiles/pub629.pdf

The Iranian, *Theatre Industry is as Alive as Film*, http://www.iranian.com/Arts/2000/January/Broadway/index.html

The White House, *The President Delivers State of the Union Address*, http://www.whitehouse.gov/news/releases/2002/01/20020129-11.html

United Nations document, http://www.un.org/documents/r55-23.pdf

Vanderbilt University, Television News Archive, ABC Evening News, *Iraq Invasion of Kuwait/ Iran*, http://openweb.tvnews.vanderbilt.edu/1990-8/1990-08-13-ABC-8.html

Government and International Organisations

Centre for Women's Participation, Office of the President, *National Report on Women's Status in the Islamic Republic of Iran*, Tehran, 2001.

Human Rights Watch/ Middle East, New York, 21 May 1997.

Educational Research and Planning Organization, *Amuzesh-e Herfeh va Fan* [Technical–Vocational Training] Tehran, Ministry of Education, 2002.

Plan and Budget Organization, Islamic Republic of Iran, *Barnameh-ye Avval-e Tose'eh Eqtesadi, Ejtema'i, Farhangi Jomhuri-ye Islami-ye Iran 1368–1372* [The First Economic, Social, Cultural Development Plan of the Islamic Republic of Iran 1989–1993], 1989.

Plan and Budget Organization, Islamic Republic of Iran, *Barnameh-ye Dovvom-e Tose'eh Eqtesadi, Ejtema'i, Farhangi Jomhuri-ye Islami-ye Iran 1373–1377* [The Second Economic, Social, Cultural Development Plan of the Islamic Republic of Iran 1994–1998], 1993.

United Nations Development Programme, *Iran: Human Development Report*, 1999.

United Nations Development Programme, *The First Millennium Development Goals Report, Islamic Republic of Iran*, 2004.

United Nations, General Assembly, *Resolution 55/2.*

United Nations, General Assembly, *United Nations Year of Dialogue Among Civilizations, Report of the Secretary General A/55/492/Rev.1.*

English Newspapers

The Economist

Financial Times

The Guardian

Hindustan Times

The Independent

International Herald Tribune

Iran Daily

Iran Times

Le Monde Diplomatique

New York Times

Tehran Times

Wall Street Journal

Persian Newspapers

Aftab-e Yazd

Azad

Ettelaat

Hamshahri

Iran

Jomhuri-ye Islami

Kayhan

Mobin

Resaalat

Salam

Shoma

Sobh-e Imruz

INDEX